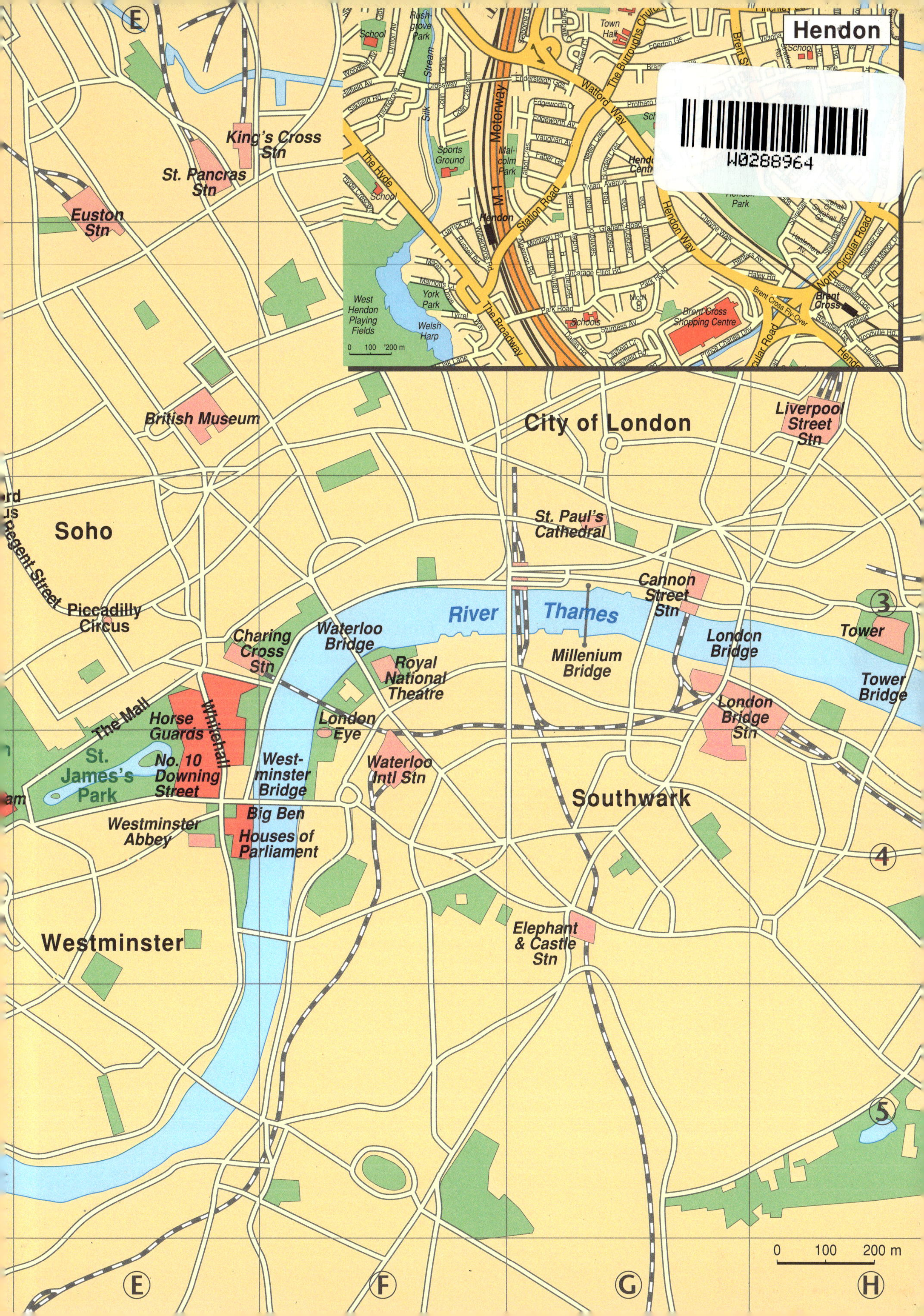

Hendon
Town Hall
The Burroughs
Watford Way
Rush-grove Park
Silk Stream
Crossway
Motorway
M 1
Sports Ground
Mal-colm Park
The Hyde
School
Hendon
Station Road
Hendon Way
Vivian Avenue
Hendon Park
North Circular Road
Brent Cross
Brent Cross Fly-Over
West Hendon Playing Fields
York Park
Welsh Harp
The Broadway
Park Road
Schools
Brent Cross Shopping Centre
0 100 200 m
E
King's Cross Stn
St. Pancras Stn
Euston Stn
British Museum
City of London
Liverpool Street Stn
Soho
Regent Street
St. Paul's Cathedral
Piccadilly Circus
Cannon Street Stn
River Thames
3
Tower
Charing Cross Stn
Waterloo Bridge
Royal National Theatre
Millenium Bridge
London Bridge
Tower Bridge
The Mall
Horse Guards
Whitehall
London Eye
London Bridge Stn
St. James's Park
No. 10 Downing Street
West-minster Bridge
Waterloo Intl Stn
Southwark
Westminster Abbey
Big Ben
Houses of Parliament
4
Westminster
Elephant & Castle Stn
5
0 100 200 m
E
F
G
H

W0288964

Dein Führerschein zum Buch

Vor dir liegt dein neues Englischbuch. Es hat unterschiedliche Teile, die dir beim Lernen helfen. Die Führerscheinaufgaben zeigen dir, wie und wo es im Buch langgeht. Versuche es doch gleich einmal. Hinter jeder Antwortmöglichkeit steht ein Buchstabe. Wenn du alle Fragen richtig beantwortet hast, erhältst du einen englischen Satz.

1 Wie heißt dein neues Englischbuch in Klasse 5?

- Portobello Road. (E)
- Portobello Road Market. (A)

2 Auf den Seiten 4-7 findest du das Inhaltsverzeichnis. Finde heraus, mit wie vielen *Themes* du dich in diesem Schuljahr beschäftigen kannst.

- Sechs. (N)
- Acht. (M)

3 Nun schau auf die Seiten 12 und 13. Hier treffen sich alle Portobello Road Kids im Park und begrüßen sich. Wie viele Kinder sind es?

- Sieben. (P)
- Sechs. (G)

4 Zeichnungen und Bilder können dir helfen, ein Thema zu verstehen. Was kannst du auf den Seiten 38 und 39 sehen?

- Ein Klassenzimmer. (K)
- Einen Supermarkt. (L)

5 Jedes *Theme* hat ein Hauptthema. Blättere die Seiten 43-56 durch. Worum geht es in *Theme* 3?

- Freizeit. (I)
- Essen und Trinken. (O)

6 Die Foto-Doppelseiten bringen dir das Leben in London näher. Was siehst du auf den Seiten 22 und 23?

- Eine U-Bahn Station. (C)
- Einen Straßenmarkt. (S)

7 In der Land & Leute-Box erfährst du mehr über das Leben in Großbritannien. Worum geht es in der Box in *Theme* 4?

- Doppeldeckerbusse. (T)
- Die Londoner U-Bahn. (H)

8 Außen an den Seiten findest du verschiedene Symbole, die dir bei der Arbeit mit dem Buch helfen, wie zum Beispiel dieses: [LiF] Was sollst du hier unter die Lupe nehmen? Tipp: Schau auf Seite 7 nach.

- Grammatik. (I)
- Ein Projekt. (W)

9 Finde dieses Zeichen: [WB] Wohin soll dich der Pfeil führen?

- Zum Wörterverzeichnis. (D)
- Zum Workbook. (S)

10 Jedes *Theme* hat eine Wortliste, in der du die Wörter findest, die ihr gerade im Unterricht besprecht. Auf welcher Seite beginnt die Wortliste für *Theme* 1?

- Seite 126. (F)
- Seite 90. (O)

11 Auf den Seiten 163-174 befinden sich Wörter, die nach dem Alphabet geordnet sind. Welche Wörter kannst du hier nachschlagen?

- Englische und deutsche. (U)
- Nur englische. (G)

12 Techniken zum Englischlernen findest du auf den *How to ...* –Seiten, die auf Seite 101 beginnen. Wie viele *How to ... –* Seiten gibt es insgesamt?

- 12 Seiten. (S)
- 9 Seiten. (N)

Hast du die Lösung gefunden? Prima!
Den Lösungssatz kannst du ganz vorne in deinem Workbook eintragen. Aber das ist noch nicht alles. In deinem Englischbuch gibt es noch viel zu entdecken. Hör dir den ersten Song auf der CD [CD] an und blättere dabei durch das Buch.
Viel Spaß mit

Portobello Road!

Inhalt

Inhalt

Inhalt

Hier kannst du dein Wissen aus der Grundschule einbringen.

extra

Hier findest du zusätzliche Übungen.

choose

Suche dir die Übung aus, die dir am besten gefällt.

Symbolerklärungen

LiF 9, 10 – Hierzu gibt es eine Erklärung im LiF-Teil.

WB 5, 6 – Hierzu gibt es Übungen im Workbook.

LiF-Ex 1,2 – Hier wird etwas geübt, was du bereits kennst. Wenn du dich unsicher fühlst, dann schlage im LiF-Teil nach.

portfolio – Du kannst diese Arbeit in deinem Portfolio-Ordner abheften.

CD – Dieser Text ist auf CD.

How to listen – Auf den *How to …* -Seiten findest du Techniken, die dir beim Englischlernen helfen.

project – Projekte sind umfangreiche Aufgaben, die ihr meist in Gruppen durchführen könnt.

Tipp
who, who, who – wer bist du?
where, where, where – wo kommst du her?

Tipps oder Hilfen

Welcome

CD

Hello everyone!
My name is Caroline Perrakis.
Perrakis is a Greek name. I'm eleven and
I have a twin brother, George. He is a clown!
We are from Manchester. We are new
in London. We live in a small house
with our mum and dad. …

My hobbies? I like inline skating,
dancing and animals. I have a cat. Her name is Socks.
She has a basket in my room. Socks likes popcorn and I
like popcorn, too. My favourite food is pizza and my favourite drink
is coke. My mum says milk is good for me – ugh, I'm not a baby!
Do you like music? I like reggae and hip hop –
I have 50 or 60 CDs. …

My new school is Hendon School.
Emma goes to Hendon School, too. She lives
in my street and she is really nice. She has a hamster.
Emma likesspaghetti and tea with milk and sugar.
My plans for tomorrow? Meeting Emma's
friends in the park.

Das kannst du schon!

✓ Du kannst schon jemanden begrüßen.
✓ Du kannst sagen, wie du heißt, wo du wohnst, wie alt du bist und was du gerne magst.
✓ Du kannst kurze englische Texte verstehen und einige englische Wörter lesen.
✓ Du kannst vielleicht auch schon einige kurze Sätze schreiben.

I like ...

I'm from ...

I'm ...

My name is ...

I have ...

My favourite ...

Tipp
Damit du möglichst viel über dich berichten kannst, schreibe künftig Wörter auf, die für dich wichtig sind. Das ist dann deine ganz **persönliche Wortliste**, die du immer weiter ergänzen kannst.

Fuzzy
Mr Batson
Grandma Williams
Mrs Perrakis
Mrs Batson
Mr Perrakis
Mrs Khan
Mr Khan
Mr Butler
Uncle Morgan
Aunt Fay
Mrs Butler
Josephine
Sheree
Mrs Williams
Mrs Collins
Gillian
David
Jack
George
Caroline
Rajiv
Sharon
Mr Williams
Emma
Charlie
Hoover
Socks

HENDON SCHOOL
Learning together across the world
HEADTEACHER
PREMISES MANAGER
F. S. FORD

1

Friends

The Royal Borough of Kensington and Chelsea
PORTOBELLO ROAD, W.11

ESTD 1887
ALICE'S
FINE ART PRINTS

OFF LICENCE
SAKIB STORES
TOP QUALITY MEATS

A1 Friends in the park

CD

a) Sing along to 'The Portobello Road Song'.

b) Look at the picture. This is Holland Park. Who can you see? What can you see? Work with a partner and find ten things.

A2 In Holland Park

CD

a) What can you hear in the park? Listen and point .

b) Now listen to the children. Who says what?

WB 1, 2

A3 Who is this?

Talk about the friends.

This is Gillian. She is from … .
… is David. He is from …

Gillian: Notting Hill

David: Hendon

…: Notting Hill

Where are the friends from?

They are all from … 

…: Hendon

…: …

…: Notting Hill

LiF 1

WB 3

CD

LiF 2

A4 Hi, what's your name?

Listen and read.

A5 What about …?

Work with a partner. Find your words for the blue words. Play the roles.

LiF 3

a an	cake orange juice coke game of football snack apple party …

WB 4-6

A6 Meeting new people

a) Listen and read.

b) Tell your partner about these people.

1. Michelle: Paris

2. Nino: Pisa

3. Selina: New York

4. Christian: Cologne

5. Murat: Istanbul

6. Andrea: Dresden

7. Tadeusz: Warsaw

8. Mandy: Sydney

9. Alexej: Moscow

CD

LiF-Ex 1

WB 7

extra

Make sentences like this.
Paris is in France.
Pisa is in … .
New York … .
…

Russia – Italy – the USA – Turkey – Germany – Australia – Poland project

portfolio

A7 Hi! I'm …

a) Write your card and hang it in the classroom.

b) Make cards with pictures of your favourite people. Write their cards like this:

c) Work with your classmates. Take a card from b) and play the role:

WB 8

LiF-Ex 2

A8 Caroline's e-mail to a friend

Read Caroline's e-mail to a friend in Manchester.

Priority: Normal

Subject: New friends

Hi Claire,
Thanks for your e-mail. How are you? :-)
London is great. I've made new friends already! Their names are Rajiv, Charlie, Emma, David and Gillian. Gillian and the boys like football. It's their favourite sport and they sometimes play in Holland Park. Gillian and Emma like reggae and hip hop, and we listen to our new CDs together. Rajiv likes music, too. He has a lot of CDs. (I must tell you: he's so nice!) Back to Emma. She reads a lot of books and comics. And it's great because they all like pets. David has a dog. His name is Hoover. Funny name, isn't it? Gillian has a cat, too. Her name is Fuzzy. Emma has a hamster. His name is Bernie. And listen to this – Charlie is president of the Holland Park School Goldfish Club! How exciting. ;-)
Well, I must finish now.

CU (( )):**
Caroline

WB 9

A9 Caroline's new friends

Read the text. Say the words for the pictures.

Caroline's new  are from London – Rajiv, David, Emma, Gillian and Charlie. Gillian and the boys like . They sometimes play in Holland . Rajiv and the girls like . They often listen to . Emma likes  and . Caroline's new friends have pets: David has a , Gillian has a , Emma has a  and Charlie has a .

A10 What you like

Say what *you* like.

I like ...    ...

WB 10, 11

choose

- **Find 8 things you like in the dictionary on pages 173-176. Write, draw and learn the words.**
- **Write about what you like.**

portfolio

B1 At a market

Tipp
Ergänze deine persönliche Wortliste.

What can you buy at a market?
Collect your words.
You can look at pages 22/23, too.

B2 In Portobello Road

How to … listen

a) Before you listen: What can you see? Make a list and tell your classmates.

I can see …

LiF 4

CD

b) Now listen to the CD. What can you hear?

c) Listen again.
Who is at the street market?
What can you buy at the street market/in Mr Khan's shop?

WB 12-14

Can you give the dog a name?

B3 Things to buy

Say what is in the shop and at the market stall.

There is a red T-shirt at the market stall.
There are blue jeans.
There is …
There are … in Mr Khan's shop.

LiF-Ex 4

LAND & LEUTE

PORTOBELLO ROAD MARKET – ein Straßenmarkt in London

Hast du schon einmal einen Straßenmarkt besucht? Dort kann man viel entdecken.

In der Portobello Road in London gibt es einen ganz berühmten Markt. Für den Verkauf von Obst und Gemüse, Snacks, gebrauchter oder billiger Kleidung ist er von Montag bis Samstag geöffnet. Samstags ist er besonders groß.

Dann werden dort auch Kunstgegenstände, Bilder und Reiseandenken verkauft. Außerdem findet man alles, was gerade *in* ist: Mode, Schmuck und tausend Kleinigkeiten. Kaum ein Londonbesucher lässt sich diesen Markt entgehen.

B4 More about Portobello Road

a) Find Notting Hill, Hendon School, Portobello Road, Holland Park, Holland Park School on the map on page 1.

Can you find more places?

b) Visit Portobello Road on the Internet.
What can you find out?
Look at: www.portobelloroad.co.uk

Tell your classmates about it.

Tipp
Finde jemanden in deiner Klasse, der dir beim Berichten helfen kann.

B5 At a market stall

It is the last day of the school holidays. Charlie and Gillian are at the market.

Can you describe them?

LiF 5

Look at Charlie. His jeans are … . He has a boat. It is … .
This is Gillian. Her bike is … . Her sunglasses are … .
There is the dog again. Its name is … . His/Her hat is … .
There is a cat, too. Its … .
Look at the children. Their clothes are … .

B6 I spy with my little eye …

Describe a boy or a girl in your class.

LiF-Ex 5

WB 15, 16

B7 Let's rap

Look at B5. Listen and rap.

Count Up

1) Say one, two – one, two.
Charlie's jeans are old and blue.

Say three, four – three, four.
Gillian's bike doesn't work any more.

Count one, two, three, four, five, six, seven
and eight, nine, ten, eleven.
Watch out for twelve!
Count the numbers one to ten
Then up to twelve and start again!

Text: Tina Toase; Music: Christian Vinzentius

2) Say five, six – five, six.
Watch the cat play funny tricks!

Say seven, eight – seven, eight.
With her glasses Gill looks great.

Count one, two, three, four, five, six, seven
and eight, nine, ten, eleven.
Watch out for twelve!
Count the numbers one to ten
Then up to twelve and start again!

3) Say nine, ten – nine, ten.
A yellow boat for two children.

Eleven, twelve – eleven, twelve
Yummy melons on a shelf.

CD

B8 A countdown

CD

WB 17, 18

a) Listen to the countdown on the CD. Say the countdown.

b) Find the number words in the rap.

c) Write the countdown in words.

B9 More numbers

a) Ask your classmates:

How old are you?

I'm ten.

b) Make a class survey.

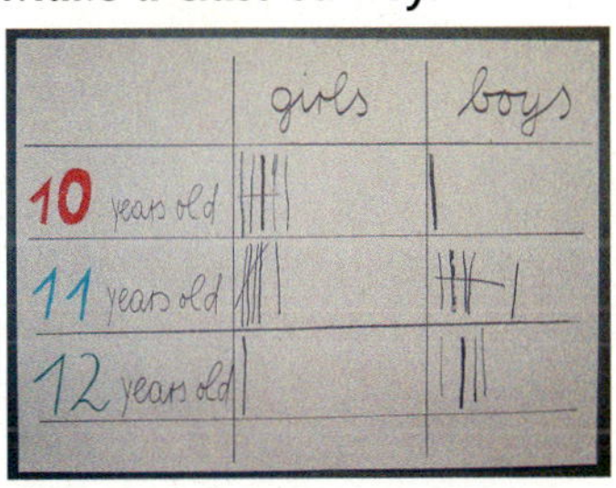

There are … boys/girls in our class. … girls/boys are … years old.

Do you have a lucky number?

My lucky number is … .

CENTRAL AVENUE
LEADING TO SOUTH HALL
VILLA mimosa
VILLA mimosa

VILLA mimosa
mimosa
JUDY
CULPEPER

C1 In Hendon School

a) Look at the classroom. Who can you see? What can you see?

WB 19, 20

CD

b) Listen to the scene in the classroom. What can you understand?

C2 School things

a) There are a lot of things in the classroom.
Work with a partner.
Say the words and point at the things on page 24.

pencil – poster – window – book – door – rubber – exercise book – felt-tip – ruler – desk – folder – computer – pen – chair – pencil case – picture – board – schoolbag

How to ... work with words

b) Ask your partner.

What's in our classroom/ your schoolbag/your pencil case?

There is .../ There are ...

Can I have ..., please?

Here you are.

What's the English/ German word for ... ?

...

Do you have ...?

No, sorry.

LiF-Ex 4

WB 21

C3 A dream classroom

Draw a picture of your dream classroom. Then label it and talk about it.

There is/There are ... in my dream classroom.

portfolio

extra

Write about your dream classroom.

C4 Kim's game

Look at the picture for 1 minute. Close your book. Write a list of the things.

CD

C5 Up to one hundred

Listen and point.

22 twenty-two · 19 nineteen · 15 fifteen · 68 sixty-eight · 16 sixteen · 14 fourteen · 47 forty-seven · 79 seventy-nine · 30 thirty · 13 thirteen · 17 seventeen · 18 eighteen · 100 one hundred · 34 thirty-four · 50 fifty · 93 ninety-three · 81 eighty-one · 20 twenty · 70 seventy · 60 sixty · 40 forty · 90 ninety · 80 eighty · 51 fifty-one

WB 22

C6 Buzz 4!

Play this game. Sit in a circle and say the numbers like this:

1 – 2 – 3 – buzz – 5 – 6 – 7 – buzz – 9 – 10 – 11 – buzz – 13 – …

Can you go on?

Tipp
Überlege dir noch mehr Zahlenspiele.

C7 The time

WB 23

Work with a partner. Ask and answer like this:

1

2

3
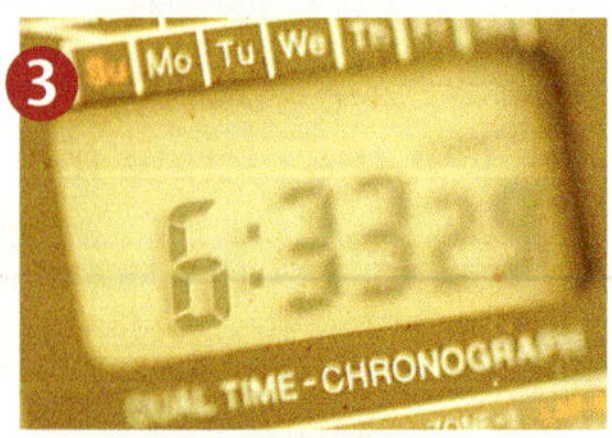

4

5

6

C8 This is me

Make a poster.

1. **Stick your photo on the poster.**
2. **Write about:**
   - **who you are,**
   - **where you are from,**
   - **how old you are,**
   - **your phone number,**
   - **what you like,**
   - **what your favourite clothes are,**
   - **what your favourite colours are.**
3. **Draw your schoolbag. What is in it?**

project

portfolio

extra

Talk about your poster and record it.

Jetzt kannst du schon viel auf Englisch machen und erzählen.

✓ Du kannst etwas über dich selbst, deine Lieblingssachen und deine Schule sagen.
✓ Du hast gelernt, wie man sich vorstellt und Sachen und Personen beschreibt.
✓ Du hast auch schon kleine Texte gelesen.
✓ Du weißt jetzt, wie du Informationen aus Hörtexten herausfinden kannst und wie du Wörter lernen kannst.

Nicht schlecht, oder?

British School Yard Games

Skipping

Say this skipping rhyme:

I like coffee, I like tea
I like Nicole to jump with me.

Please Mr Crocodile

Play this game with four or five friends.
One person is 'Mr Crocodile' and the other people say "Please Mr Crocodile can we cross your Golden River." Mr Crocodile replies with something like "Only if you are wearing something blue."
If you are wearing that colour, you can move on one step. When you reach the other side, you are then the next 'Mr Crocodile'.

Conkers – a favourite children's game

A lot of British children play it in September and October.

Play it with a friend. You must hit your partner's conker hard. Take it in turns. The best conker wins.
Find out more about the conker game rules:
http://www.bbc.co.nk/norfolk/kids/conkers_3.shtml

Clapping rhymes

Clap your hands with a partner and say a rhyme.

A sailor went to
sea, sea, sea.
To see what he could
see, see, see.
But all that he could
see, see, see.
Was the bottom of the deep blue
sea, sea, sea.

I went to a Chinese restaurant
To buy a loaf of bread.
They asked me what my name was,
And this is what I said:
My name is E.I., E.I. Nickeleye, Nickeleye
Pom pom poodle, willy willy whiskers.
My name is
FREEZE.

2

A good start

GOOD MORNI

A1 Good morning

WB 1

Find morning words.

A2 In the bathroom

CD

a) Look at the pictures and listen to the CD. Point to the body parts you can hear.

LiF 6

WB 2

b) Right or wrong?

1. David is in the bathroom at 8 o'clock.
2. David's mother is in the bathroom.
3. Breakfast is on the table.
4. David likes water in the swimming pool.
5. David's mother must go shopping.

Yes, that's right.

No, that's wrong.

c) Read the story again. Act the scene.

A3 Sound check

Look at these words and say them.
Make two lists: one for [iː] and one for [e].

be – teeth – pen – feet
red – neck – sea – we

[iː]	[e]
green	*yes*
...	...

NG EVERYONE!

A4 Boys and girls

These are the parts of the body.

a) Look at the parts of the body. Make a list like this:

one	two or more
face	*hands*
head	…
…	

b) What do you notice? Write another list like this:

one	*two or more*
leg	*legs*
…	*hands*
…	…

LiF-Ex 6

How to ... work with grammar

WB 3-7

A5 The washing song

Listen to the song and act it.

In the morning, what do I see?
In the mirror, can that be me?
My hair up straight on top of my head.
My eyes are half open.
What's that Mum said?

Chorus:
Take your toothbrush, toothpaste and hairbrush.
Take your comb and soap from your toilet bag and wash!
Washing, washing, boy, it's neat.
Hair and face and hands and feet.
Washing, washing, ev'ry day, rinsing all the dirt away.

In the evening, it's time for bed.
In the mirror, my eyes are red.
My hair's so dirty. Where's the shampoo?
My teeth are furry. What should I do?

Take your toothbrush, toothpaste and …

Text: Frank van Ruyssevelt
Music: Wolfgang Hering and Brigitte Schanz-Hering

choose

- **Find all the body words in the song. Write them in an alphabetical list.**
- **Find all the things in a bathroom. Write about them.**

  The toothbrush is for my teeth. The soap is …

A6 I hate the bathroom

David is still in the bathroom.

What's that?
A big nose, big ears
and long black teeth?
Hmm. No, I'm not so ugly.
I'm not a monster.

Wow, what a
good-looking guy!
His hair is blond and
his eyes are blue.
He's tall and strong.
But I'm not Tarzan.

Grrr! Slim body, short brown hair,
dark eyes and a small nose.
Oh! That's me!
Hi, Mr Perfect.

WB 8

a) Which words describe the monster, Tarzan, David? Which words describe **you**? Write down the words like this:

monster	Tarzan	David	me
big nose	good-looking		

Tipp
Suche weitere Wörter aus dem *dictionary* heraus.

b) **Talk about yourself:** That's me.
You can start your sentences like this:

I have …
My ears are …
My nose is …
I'm …
I'm not …

extra

Write about yourself and draw a picture.

portfolio

A7 People

Look at page 10 and listen to the CD. Who are the people?

CD

choose

- **Describe other people on page 10 to a partner.**
- **Write about the people on page 10.**

…	is	the	tall short slim big old …	man woman girl boy	with	long short	red black brown blond grey straight …	hair.

WB 9, 10

A8 A poem

a) **Read the poems.**

Hair
blond hair
short blond hair
my brother Philipp.

A girl
a tall girl
a tall slim girl
my cousin Maybel

b) **Write your poem and present it to the class. You can write about a classmate, a friend or someone in your family.**

portfolio

B1 What's for breakfast?

WB 11

It is breakfast time.
What can you have for breakfast?
Make a list like this:

breakfast	
food	drink
...	...

B2 Breakfast for Mum

CD

It is Saturday morning. Gillian is in the dining-room.

Mum: Mmh, is that coffee? Where are you?

LiF 7

Gillian: I'm here. Come on, breakfast is ready!
Mum: Oh! Am I late?
Gillian: No, you aren't. It's Saturday!
Mum: Oh yes. Great. Mmm, coffee. Is the milk on the table? The sugar?

Gillian: Yup. And bacon and eggs.
Mum: Super. Can I have baked beans, too?
Gillian: Yes – and a sausage. And toast.
Mum: Where's the marmalade? Still in the cupboard?
Gillian: Oops, yes, it is. One moment.

Mum: Gillian, this is really great. A super breakfast. Thank you.

Gillian: Hey, Mum. It's Saturday. Let's go shopping.
Mum: Well, Gillian …

WB 12, 13

a) Can you finish the story?

b) Write new breakfast words in your list from B1. What are the words in German? Practise with a partner.

What's sugar in German?

It's ... .

Land & Leute

ENGLISCHES FRÜHSTÜCK

Ein traditionelles englisches Frühstück ist schon etwas Besonderes!
Es beginnt mit einem Glas Orangensaft oder einer halben Grapefruit. Dann isst man Cornflakes, Haferflocken oder andere Getreideflocken (auf Englisch *cereal*) mit Milch.

Es folgt ein warmes Gericht, z.B. gebratener Schinkenspeck mit Ei, kleine Bratwürstchen mit Bohnen in Tomatensauce und Grilltomaten und gebratene Pilze (auf Englisch *mushrooms*).

Außerdem gibt es Toast mit Butter und Orangenmarmelade (auf Englisch *marmalade*, andere Marmelade heißt *jam*).

Dazu trinkt man schwarzen Tee mit Milch oder Kaffee.

Allerdings ist für so ein ausgiebiges Frühstück auch in englischen Familien oft nur am Wochenende Zeit. Während der Woche, wenn alle arbeiten und zur Schule gehen, lassen viele Familien das warme Gericht weg.

B3 Gillian's breakfast

**Look at the text and the pictures in B2 again.
Can you find the answers?**

Is Gillian in the dining-room?
Is it Monday?
Are the milk and sugar on the table?
Is the toast on the table?
Is the marmalade on the table?
Are the bacon and eggs in the cupboard?
Is Gillian's mother late?
Is the coffee on the table?

No, it isn't. Yes, she is.
Yes, it is. No, they aren't.
No, it isn't. Yes, it is.
Yes, they are. No, she isn't.

LiF-Ex 7

WB 14

B4 Your breakfast

a) Make a class survey. Write down what you have for breakfast. Draw pictures for the words you can't write in English. Hang the poster in your classroom.

b) Talk about your breakfast with your classmates.

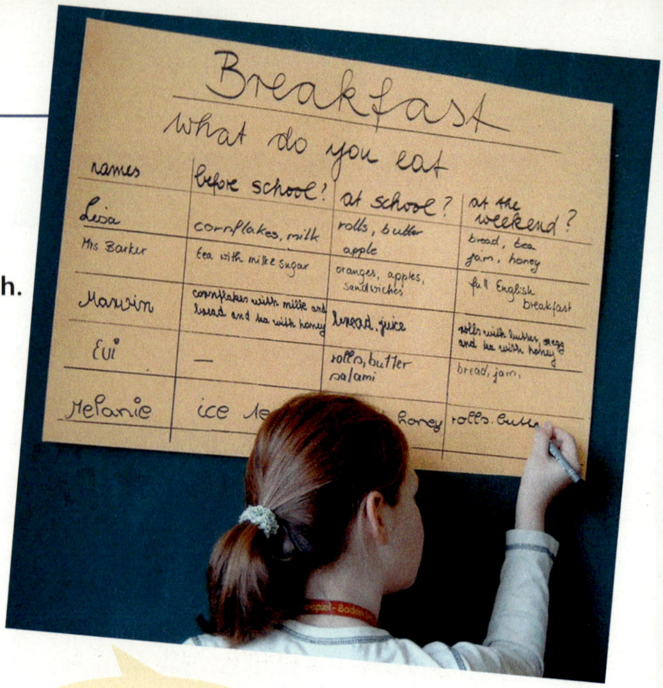

What do you eat before school?

Before school, I eat …

What do you have for breakfast at the weekend?

At the weekend, I have …

What do you eat at school?

At school, I eat …

B5 My breakfast

In an e-mail to the partner school in Sweden Charlie writes about his breakfast.

a) Read Charlie's e-mail.

WB 15, 16

Priority: Normal

Subject: My breakfast

What we eat

Education and Culture
Socrates
Comenius

My breakfast:
I have breakfast at eight o'clock. I like cornflakes with milk and sugar for breakfast. I like toast and marmalade. I don't like eggs and bacon for breakfast. I like tea. My sister Josephine has coffee for breakfast. That's all. She has a sandwich at work and an apple or an orange. But I like breakfast in the kitchen.

(Charlie Batson)

My breakfast:

portfolio

Tipp
Denke an Uhrzeit, Essen Getränke, Ort.

b) Write about your breakfast.

B6 Tarzan's breakfast

a) **Read the recipe and look at the pictures. Write the shopping list.**

shopping list
butter
...
...

1 Preheat oven to 180° C.
2 Put some butter in a cake pan.
3 Cut an apple and put it in the cake pan with sugar and cinnamon.
4 Beat two eggs with 75ml milk.
5 Add 50g of flour.
6 Cover the apples with the mixture.
7 Bake for 15 minutes.
8 Eat with yoghurt.

b) **Make Tarzan's breakfast for your class.**

What's your superduper breakfast?

C1 In the supermarket

What can you buy in your supermarket?

C2 Shopping

It is Friday afternoon. Here is David in the supermarket.

a) Listen to the CD. Follow David's way through the supermarket.

CD

LiF 8

David: Aha! The yoghurt is next to the milk. The cheese … and the butter are over there. Ah, yes. Cornflakes … good … and the bread? The bread, where's the bread? Ah, I can see it. Now, onions. Vegetables … vegetables … Where are the vegetables?
Shop assistant: Can I help you?
David: Yes, please. Where are the vegetables?
Shop assistant: There they are. Right behind you. Next to the door.
David: OK, so onions … and apples. Now orange juice. Aaah! Three bottles. … Eggs … Where are the eggs? …
Excuse me. Where are the eggs?
Shop assistant: See the lady? She's in front of them.
David: Thank you. OK. … And chips, frozen chips. The freezer, the freezer. Ah! There it is. OK. And what about a magazine for me? I'm sure mum wouldn't mind.

b) What is on David's shopping list?

C3 What's where?

a) Look at the picture. Talk about the supermarket.

The chips The milk The apples The lady David The shop assistant …	is are	on in next to behind in front of …	the onions. the butter. the yoghurt. the freezer. the eggs. the orange juice. …

WB 17, 18

LiF-Ex 8

b) Now ask your partner:

What / Who is next to …? / behind …? / in front of …? / …

C4 Things in my trolley

Play the shopping game.

WB 19, 20

LAND & LEUTE

BRITISCHES GELD

In Großbritannien wird mit *pounds* und *pence* bezahlt. Für das *pound* gibt es dieses Zeichen: £. Das ist eigentlich ein L; es steht für *libra*, das lateinische Wort für Pfund.

Diese Geldscheine findet ihr: £5, £10, £20, £50. *Pence* werden mit p abgekürzt; es gibt diese Münzen: 1p, 2p, 5p, 10p, 20p, 50p, £1, £2. Ein *pound* hat 100 *pence*.

Erkundigt euch, wie viel £1 in Euro ist. Wie viel bekommt ihr für 10p, 20p, 50p? Könnt ihr euer Taschengeld in *pounds* und *pence* umrechnen?

WB 21

SPECIAL OFFERS

In britischen Geschäften sind *special offers* (Sonderangebote) sehr beliebt. Versucht herauszufinden, welche Angebote auf den beiden Fotos gemacht werden.

C5 How much ...?

a) What can you see? Make a list like this and add new words:

food + drink	school things	clothes
...	...	...
...	...	...

How to ... work with words

WB 22

b) Can you say the prices? Talk to a partner:

How much are the apples?

They're £1 a kilo.

How much is the pullover?

It's £8 .

c) Make posters with prices for a class supermarket.

C6 At the baker's

CD

a) Read the roles with a partner.

b) Use your posters from C5 for more shopping dialogues.

Jetzt hast du schon eine Menge gelernt.
✓ Du kannst dich selbst und andere beschreiben.
✓ Du kannst über deine Frühstücksgewohnheiten sprechen und schreiben.
✓ Du kannst beschreiben, wo sich Dinge oder Personen befinden.
✓ Du kannst kurze Einkaufsgespräche führen.
✓ Du hast gelernt, wie du neue Wörter zum Lernen organisieren kannst.
✓ Du hast gelernt, wie du selbst etwas über Grammatik herausfinden kannst.
Das ist doch klasse, oder?

Optional

1. Crazy friends

- Make a crazy friend. Make a collage. Describe it to a partner.

- Then write about your friend.
- Collect all collages and hang them in your classroom.

2. Crazy words

Look at the two pictures.

traffic jam

Draw crazy pictures for these words.

hands of the clock

fish fingers

black eye

3

Free time

HOLLAND
PARK
SCHOOL

CLUBS
P.E. DEPARTMENT ACTIVITIES
YOUNG WOMAN'S DAY

A1 What's your hobby?

WB 1, 2

A2 At Holland Park School

a) Find all the hobbies on the noticeboard.

b) Can you find more information?

A3 Holland Park School Cup Final

Look at the noticeboard. Find out about the cup final.

sport	There is a …
place	The cup final is at …
day	It is on …
time	It is at …

LiF 9, 10

A4 More about the cup final

CD

Look at the picture and listen to the CD. Match the right answers to the questions.

1. Who is in the cup final?
2. Is the cup final for boys and girls?
3. What can the girls have?
4. Who can watch the final?
5. When is the final?
6. Where is the cup final?
7. What can everyone bring to the final?

a. On Saturday, at 10:30.
b. A friendly match.
c. Family and friends.
d. A school scarf.
e. At Hendon School.
f. No, only for boys.
g. Holland Park School and Hendon School.

Tipp
who, who, who – wer bist du?
where, where, where – wo kommst du her?

extra

a) Look at the noticeboard. Which notice is interesting for you?

WB 3, 4

b) Work with a partner. Write a notice. Collect the notices and hang them on a noticeboard in your classroom.

project

CD

A5 The friendly match

It is Friday. Gillian phones Emma about the friendly match the next day …

a) What is Emma's problem?

Emma: 7578063. Hello?
Gillian: Hi, Emma. This is Gillian.
Emma: Hello, Gillian. What's up?
Gillian: Listen. I have eleven girls on my team now. We can play tomorrow. I can't wait! I'm so excited.
Emma: Er, wow. Mmh, good for you. Er, …
Gillian: What's wrong? What about your team?
Emma: Well, there's a problem. Mary has a cold and can't come.
Gillian: Oh dear. I'm sorry. What can we do? Can you ask Caroline?
Emma: Caroline? Well, can she play? She likes inline skating – but football?
Gillian: She can run fast and …
Emma: Yes, well, OK then. Why not? We need one more girl.
Gillian: Great. I'm sure she's a good player. See you tomorrow. Bye.
Emma: Well, OK then. Bye.

LiF-Ex 9

b) What do you know about the girls?

Gillian Emma Mary Caroline The girls	can can't	play. come. ask Caroline. wait. run fast. …

WB 5-7

LiF-Ex 10

A6 The boys and girls

What can you say about the boys and girls? Describe them. Look at pages 45-46 for more ideas.

Emma Brenda Gillian Rajiv The children The boy	has have	three school scarves. a blue T-shirt. red hair. …

A7 Change places

Sit in a circle. One boy/girl is in the middle. He/She can ask questions like these:

Start again:

Who has …
… eyes?
… for breakfast?
a/an … T-shirt?
… shoes?
a bike?
a computer?
…

LAND & LEUTE

FOOTBALL

Das Fußballspiel wurde in England erfunden und es ist dort ebenso beliebt wie bei uns. Sogar in kleinen Vereinen gibt es gut organisierte Gruppen von Fans. Sie ziehen zu allen Spielen „ihres" Clubs mit und feuern ihn an. Dabei tragen sie meistens die Farben ihres Vereins.

Übrigens: Wenn Engländer von *football* sprechen, meinen sie dasselbe wie wir mit „Fußball". Wenn Amerikaner das Wort gebrauchen, meinen sie *American football*, Neuseeländer meinen *rugby*. „Unser" Fußballspiel heißt dort *soccer*. (Diese Bezeichnung wird auch in England verstanden.)

Kennt ihr die Regeln für *American football* oder *rugby*? Versucht doch einmal, etwas mehr darüber zu erfahren. Hier sind einige nützliche Internetadressen:

Rugby: www.planet-rugby.com
American football: www.football.com; www.kids-american-football.de

A8 School teams

a) Read Gillian's e-mail to her partner school in Sweden.

Hi! I'm Gillian. I like football a lot. We have two football teams at my school – a team for the boys and a team for the girls. We all have red T-shirts and blue shorts. We wear white socks and black football boots. Mr Green has a black kit. He is our coach. Jessica is our goalkeeper. Training is after school on Wednesdays. My favourite team is Chelsea. What about your school teams? CU, Gillian.

Education and Culture
Socrates
Comenius

b) Write about your school team or your favourite team.

portfolio

WB 8, 9

A9 The football chant

Listen and read.

Let's play football –
Football is great!
Can you run fast?
I'm not the last!

Put on your shorts!
My new black shorts.
Put on your boots!
Here are my boots.

Kick and run!
This is fun!
Kick the ball!
Let's do it all!

CD

choose

- **Learn the chant and support your favourite team at the next match.**
- **Write a new chant about your favourite sport or your hobby.**

portfolio

B1 Emma and Caroline on the phone

CD

Listen to Emma and Caroline.
Then read and write the dialogue.

B2 The next match

When is your next match?
Talk to a partner.
Look at B1 for help.

Hello?

Hi …
It's me, … Listen,
……. there's …….
……. Can you
come/play?

……. ?
What time?

……. .

Well, yes.
I can.

No, sorry.
I can't.

Super.
See you.

Oh no.

How to … talk

the cup final
a football match
a tennis match
a hockey match
a streetball match
a handball match
…

at our school
in the park
at the playing fields
at the sports centre
on the tennis court
in the gym
…

on Saturday
Sunday
Monday
Tuesday
Wednesday
Thursday
Friday

at 9:30
10:00
10:30
…

LiF 11

WB 10, 11

B3 And the winner is …

a) Look at the pictures before you read. Who are the winners and who are the losers? Why?

How to … read

Netscape
http://www.hollandpark.kensington-chelsea.sch.uk/

News: Fantastic match for Holland Park girls

On Saturday Holland Park girls beat Hendon girls 3:1 in a friendly match. at Hendon School Gillian Collins (2) and Brenda Tan Fong (1) scored the goals. It was a great match.

A fair match in the cup final at Hendon School

Hendon School boys' team won the match 2:1 against the Holland Park team on Saturday. Ron Scott scored in the last minute. It was a great match.
Better luck next year, boys …!

b) Read the football reports. What are they about?

c) Are the sentences right or wrong?

1. Hendon girls were the winners.
2. Brenda scored two goals.
3. The girls' match was great.
4. The boys' cup final was fair.
5. The boys from Hendon School were the losers.
6. The score of the girls' match was 2:1.

That's right.

That's wrong.

B4 Football words

a) Find the football words on pages 45-49. Write them in English and then in German.

How to … work with words

b) Make a mindmap and organize your words. Can you find more words?

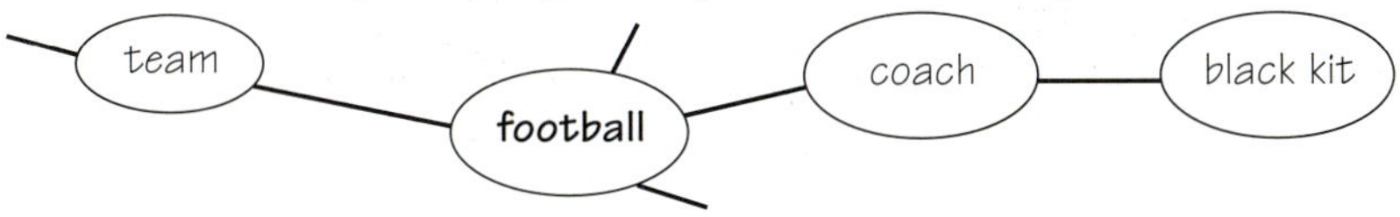

WB 12, 13

c) Kick out the footballs:

The boys' team had a ⚽⚽⚽ on Saturday. – ⚽⚽⚽ = match

1. Holland Park girls played ⚽⚽⚽ Hendon girls.
2. The girls had black ⚽⚽⚽.
3. The ⚽⚽⚽ of the cup is Hendon School.
4. There were eleven boys or girls in a ⚽⚽⚽.
5. Hendon boys won the ⚽⚽⚽.
6. The matches were at ⚽⚽⚽.
7. The matches were ⚽⚽⚽.
8. Hendon girls were the ⚽⚽⚽.

Tipp
Ergänze deine persönliche Wortliste.

B5 Can you do it?

LiF-Ex 9

a) Ask your classmates.

Can you ...?

Yes, of course.

No, I can't.

Yes, a little.

... speak English?

... speak Italian?

... speak Turkish?

... speak Russian?

... speak Polish?

... play streetball?

... tell a joke in English?

... play the keyboard?

... wiggle your ears?

... ride a unicycle?

... make a pizza?

... do 10 press-ups?

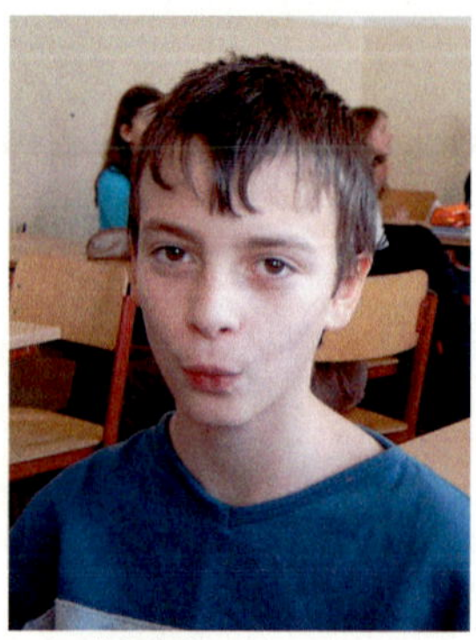
... whistle?

... ?

b) Make a class survey.

B6 Activities

a) Work with a partner. Ask and answer like this.

Where can you …?

Well, you can ride your bike in …

Where can you	play	football handball basketball tennis table tennis streetball badminton hockey riding	
You can	go	swimming inline skating	on a playing field. at a sports centre. in a swimming pool. in a park. in a gym. on a tennis court. at home. in the street.
	do	judo karate	
	ride	a bike a horse	

project

LiF-Ex 9, 11

Tipp
Viele Sportarten heißen im Deutschen und Englischen ähnlich.

WB 16

b) What about you? Talk to a partner.

Is there a sports centre/ … club near you?

Yes, there is. It's in … Street.

Yes, it's called … .

No, there isn't.

What do they wear?

They wear …

Are you a member?

Yes, I am.

No, I'm not.

C1 Puzzle it out

WB 17

a) Do you know these animals and pets?

c _ t   sp _ d _ r   t _ g _ r   r _ bb _ t   f _ sh   d _ g   h _ dgeh _ g   cr _ c _ d _ l _

b) What do you know about them?

A … can live in a … .
A … isn't a pet.
A … can't live in a … .
A … is a pet.

C2 A wild animal?

CD

WB 18

Look at the pictures and listen. Who is Henrietta?

C3 Henrietta

What can you find out about Henrietta? Match the parts.

1. Gillian, Charlie and Rajiv
2. Gillian can see
3. A hedgehog can
4. Gillian can't
5. The name of the hedgehog
6. Henrietta is
7. Gillian can
8. Gillian's mum is

a. give Henrietta some water.
b. eat snails.
c. a hedgehog on the road.
d. not happy about Henrietta.
e. are in the park.
f. is Henrietta.
g. bring the hedgehog into the flat.
h. a wild animal.

WB 19

C4 Can you take a goldfish to school?

Write about animals and pets.

I can't But I can	take keep	a an	hedgehog dog goldfish elephant bird …	to the swimming pool. to school. in the house. in an aquarium. in a shoe box. in a basket. in a cage.

LiF-Ex 9, 11

extra

Can you write some funny sentences, too? Read them to a partner.

C5 Can I …?

Work with a partner. Ask and answer.

LiF-Ex 9

WB 20

Can I	have a/an	+ 	+ 	…	?
	play	− 	…	+ 	?
	go to the	…	+ 	− 	?

C6 Pets

CD

Listen to Gillian and Charlie.
What pets do they have? Talk about them.
Gillian has a …
Her name is …
She can …

Charlie has a pet. It is …
It can't …
I think Charlie has …

C7 Pet questions

WB 21, 22

a) Match the answers to the questions. Then read with a partner.

Do you have a pet?
What is it?
What is its name?
Is he big?
What colour is he?

He's dark brown.
It's a dog. A dachshund.
Yes.
It's a he. His name is Sammy.
No, he's very small. He looks like a sausage.

b) Talk to a partner about your pet or dream pet.

C8 My dream pet or animal

My dream animal is a pony. Oh, I would love a pony. A dark brown pony. A Shetland pony. They are very small. We can ride together in the park. My pony's name can be Sandy. She can be my best friend. She can't live in my room. She has her own stable. I can give her carrots when she does tricks. Yes – a pony is my dream animal.

portfolio

Write about your dream pet or animal.

C9 An animal quiz

Play this game with two teams. Ask questions to find out about the animal. Count your questions. The team with the least questions is the winner.

Do you have a pet? — Yes.

Is it big?
Can it swim?
Can it fly?
Can it walk?
Is it a cat?

Yes, it is.
No, it isn't.

Yes, it can.
No, it can't.

LiF-Ex 7, 9

WB 23

Auch in diesem *Theme* hast du wieder eine Menge dazugelernt.

- ✓ Du kannst Fragen über Sport, Hobbys und Tiere stellen und du kannst dich über deine Freizeit unterhalten.
- ✓ Du kannst höflich um Erlaubnis bitten.
- ✓ Du hast gelernt, wie man ein kurzes Telefongespräch führt.
- ✓ Du weißt jetzt auch, wie du Informationen aus kurzen Lesetexten herausfinden und wie du noch besser Wörter lernen kannst

Super! Mach weiter so!

1. Your new pet

portfolio

Make a care sheet for a pet.

++ VET 4 PETS ++

I have a new hamster. Do you have some tips for me?

Dr Jane West

So you have a new hamster? Hamsters like to play. Give your hamster a wheel to run in. They like clean cages and a soft place to sleep. Make sure your hamster has a lot of fresh water and fresh food. Carrots or apples are good for your hamster. Be careful when you take your hamster out of its cage. Hamsters are night animals so put the cage in a safe place at night – not in your room. Your hamster will wake you up ...

2. About pets

Read about the pets. What can you understand?

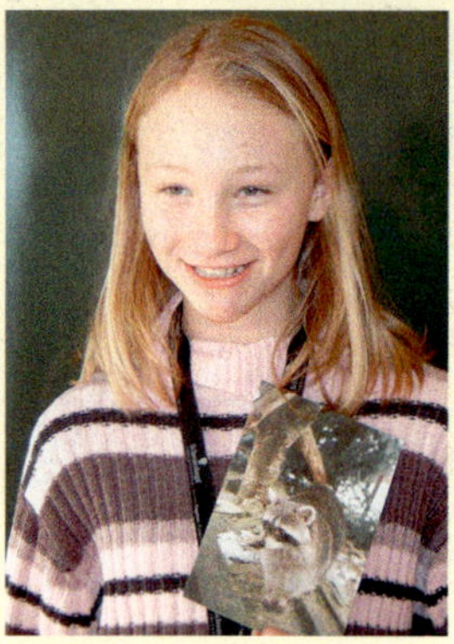

My raccoon Max
I have a lovely black and white raccoon. His name is Max. He is three years old. We got him from an animal sanctuary. His favourite food is cornflakes with milk. He has very good eyes and can see in the dark. He has a cage in our garden. I play with him in the afternoons.

MC spider
My pet is a spider. Don't worry – he is very nice.
A lot of people say spiders are ugly – that's not true. His name is MC spider. He is a lovely black colour. His favourite food is beetles and he can run very fast. I have a terrarium for him in my room.

3. About mice

Mice

I think mice
are rather nice.
Their tails are long,
their faces small,
they haven't any chins at all.

Their ears are pink,
their teeth are white,
they run about the house at night.

They nibble things
they shouldn't touch
and no one seems
to like them much.

But I think mice
are nice.

© Rose Fyleman

portfolio

- Find the rhyming words in the poem.
- Write **your** own poem.

4

The way we live

A1 What's in your room?

There is a/an … in my room.

I have …

There are … in my room.

Tipp
Ergänze deine persönliche Wortliste.

A2 In Caroline's room

What can you see in Caroline's room?
There is …
There are …
Caroline has …

WB 1

What can you say about her?
Caroline likes …
She plays with …

A3 A weekend visit

CD

a) Listen to the CD. Then read the text.

Caroline is in her room. She wants to invite Gillian for a sleepover this weekend. …

WB 2

Caroline: Listen, Gillian. Do you want to come this afternoon and stay the night? I have an extra bed in my room. You can sleep there.
Gillian: Oh, yes. That's a great idea. What's your room like? Is it big?
Caroline: Well, not really but I like it. There's a desk with a chair and a wardrobe. And a small table under the window. And then I have two shelves for my games and books. And a bed, of course. Oh, and a shelf for my CDs. My CD player is on a small table.
Gillian: Oh great. I can bring my new CDs.
Caroline: Good idea! We can have a great chat. Is two thirty OK?
Gillian: Yes, two thirty is fine.
Caroline: See you at the station then. Well, I must tidy up my room now. It's eleven o'clock already.
Gillian: Just a minute. I forgot to tell you …

b) What is it?

You can sleep there.
You can play your CDs in it.
You can put your clothes in it.
You can put your books on it.
You can do your homework at it.

WB 3-6

A4 Where are Caroline's things?

a) Work with a partner. Play this game.

books – CDs – inline skates – school uniform – …

LiF-Ex 8

b) Write about Caroline's room.

The	pencil case	is	behind	the	shelf.
	jeans	are	on		desk.
	ruler		under		chair.
	elephants		in		wardrobe.
	…		next to		bed.
			in front of		table.
					extra bed.
					window.

Tipp
Nicht vergessen:

CD

A5 Who's untidy?

1

Socks on the table
Jeans on the floor.
Look under your books
For CDs and more.

George, your twin brother
Can help you, says mother.

2

Watch out now, dear sister.
'Cause here comes 'Big Mister'!
I'm really quite strong,
So it won't take us long.

No, thank you, dear brother,
I can do this alone.
I can tidy up my room –
And you do your own!

3

And what is all this now
Under my bed?
Ah, my books and my elephant,
In my favourite red.

So into the wardrobe
With all of this here
And now I am ready –
My room is now clear!

WB 7

a) Listen and read. Who is untidy? What do you think?

b) Work in groups of three and act the scene.

Now Caroline's room is tidy. But where is her cat, Socks?

A6 My room – your room

In an e-mail to a friend in Manchester, George tells him about his life in London – and his new room.

a) Read about George's room.

London? I like it here in London. The school is great and I have a lot of new friends. The house is OK, too. Best thing is my room. It's great. I have a new wardrobe for my clothes. There's a new shelf, too, for all my CDs. There are posters on the walls. My computer is on a desk. I keep my sports gear in a big box. My mum says I can have friends to stay. You can come and stay in the holidays. We can

How to ... write

b) Write about *your* room. These beginnings can help you:

portfolio

My room is ...

I have ...

I keep ... in/on/under ...

There is/are ...

There is/are ... on the walls.

B1 Busy family

CD

At Caroline's home, everyone is busy on Saturday mornings.

First, Caroline's dad always does the shopping. Then he cooks a delicious moussaka.

Caroline's mum cleans the windows and then sets the table for lunch.

Caroline helps her dad in the kitchen – she does the washing up. Then she goes to her room, makes her bed and tidies up.

Her brother, George, tidies up the living room. He hoovers the carpet and waters the plants. Caroline and George don't like these jobs.

And Socks? Socks watches TV.

Find out who does what.

Who …

- … cooks moussaka?
- … waters the plants?
- … does the shopping?
- … tidies up the living room?
- … does the washing up?
- … cleans the windows?
- … makes her bed?
- … sets the table?
- … tidies up her room?
- … watches TV?
- … hoovers the carpet?

LiF 12, 15

WB 8-11

B2 Things to do

a) Match the words.

tidy up	the carpet
make	the bed
do	the washing up
clean	the windows
water	homework
set	the room
hoover	the living room
watch	the plants
…	the table
	the shopping
	TV
	…

b) What do you do at home? What don't you do? Make a list like this.

+	–
do the washing up	*set the table*
	hoover the living room

Write about what you do/don't do at home.

I do the washing up. *I don't set the table.*

… …

LiF-Ex 12, 15

B3 On the tube

It is a long way to Hendon and Gillian takes the tube. She gets on the tube at Westbourne Park Station, changes trains at Kings Cross St. Pancras and gets off at Hendon Central.

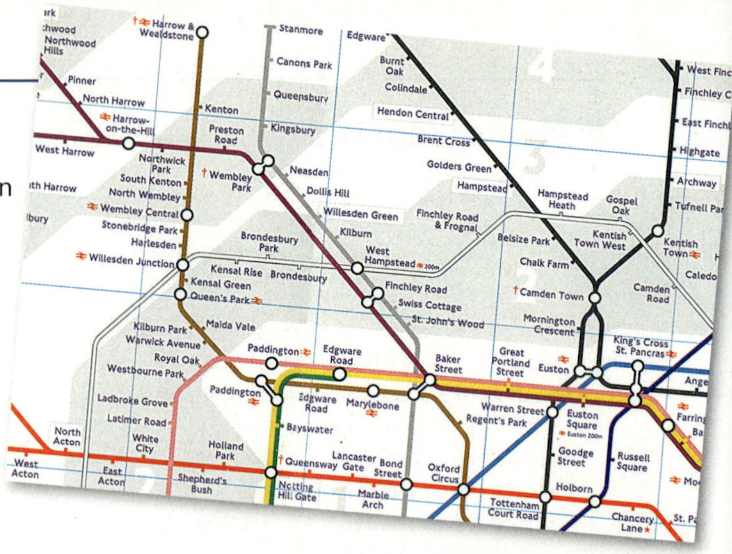

a) **What does the word 'tube' mean?**

WB 12, 13

b) **Find Westbourne Park Station and Hendon Central.**

c) **How many stations are there on Gillian's way?**

B4 Saturdays in Hendon

CD

a) **Listen to the CD. Say what you can hear.**

It is almost two thirty. Gillian gets off the train and meets Caroline at the exit. It is very cold and there is some snow. The girls walk to Caroline's house.

On the way they see Mr Coggins. He always sells hot chestnuts in winter. The girls buy some. Oops! A snowball. Poor Mr Coggins drops the bag of chestnuts, but the girls pick them up. They are still warm. Mmh.

WB 14

And there is Tony, Caroline's neighbour. He works in the Pizza Palace on Saturdays. Now he has three pizzas in his arms. Oops! Another snowball. Poor Tony. He drops his pizzas. The girls help him and pick up the boxes. They are warm, too.

The girls talk about their plans for Sunday. Cinema or the youth club or a walk in the park – Caroline has a lot of ideas for an exciting weekend.

Snowball number three! This time poor Caroline has snow on her head! And that's not warm at all!

They meet Socks in front of Caroline's house. She is cold, too. She doesn't like the snow. Caroline opens the door and Socks runs in. The girls follow. Caroline's parents are there.

b) Read the text. What do these people do?

Gillian … Caroline … The girls …

They … Socks … Tony … Mr Coggins …

LiF-Ex 12

c) Put the words in the correct order.

1. train – gets off – the – Gillian.
2. in winter – sells – hot chestnuts – Mr Coggins – always.
3. drops – Tony – pizzas – his.
4. exciting weekend – a lot of – has – Caroline – ideas – for an.
5. the snow – doesn't – Socks – like.
6. in front of – meet – The girls – Socks – Caroline's house.

LAND & LEUTE

DIE LONDONER U-BAHN

Warst du schon einmal in einer Großstadt wie Frankfurt, Berlin oder Hamburg? Dann hast du gesehen, dass es dort sehr geschäftig zugeht: Autos, Lastwagen, Busse und Taxis verstopfen die Straßen, Fußgänger rennen, bummeln, kaufen ein …
Oft kommt man schneller voran, wenn man mit der U-Bahn fährt.

London hat die älteste U-Bahn der Welt. Die Londoner haben ihr einen lustigen Namen gegeben: *tube* – Röhre. Am 9. Januar 1863 wurde die Metropolitan Line eröffnet. Sie war die erste Strecke und führte von Farringdon bis Paddington. Damals zogen Dampfloks die unterirdischen Züge.

Tipp
Aktuelle Infos zur Londoner U-Bahn findest du im Internet unter *www.tube.tfl.gov.uk/tfl*

Heute besteht das Streckennetz aus 13 Linien mit einer Gesamtlänge von 400 km. Der längste Tunnel ist 27 km lang. Die längste Rolltreppe (in Angel Station) führt 60 m in die Tiefe. Das entspricht etwa einem Hochhaus mit 20 Stockwerken.

GREASE
THE CAMBRIDGE THEATRE
Euston Oxford Street
Marble Arch Park Lane
Hyde Park Corner
Knightsbridge Kensington
G'S CROSS
GREASE
THE CAMBRIDGE THEATRE
Please
GIVE WAY
to the bus

C885 BYM
BUS

B5 Meeting Caroline's parents

CD

Find out Caroline's family name.
What are the first names of Caroline's parents?

Caroline: Come and meet my parents. Dad, this is Gillian!
Gillian: Hello. Nice to meet you.
Mr Perrakis: Hi, Gillian. How are you?
Gillian: Fine, Mr Perrakis. Thank you.
Mr Perrakis: No, not Mr Perrakis. Just call me Nikos.
Caroline: And this is my mum.
Mrs Perrakis: Hello, Gillian. Call me Amy, dear.
Gillian: Yes, Mrs Perr … er – Amy. Thank you.
Mr Perrakis: What about some hot chocolate?
You must be very cold.
Caroline: Mmh, great idea!
Gillian: Hot chocolate is my favourite drink in winter.

LiF 13

WB 15, 16

choose

- **Act the scene. Work in groups of four: Mr and Mrs Perrakis, Caroline and Gillian.**
- **Work in groups of four: two parents, two children. Now introduce your friend.**

Nice to meet you.

Fine, thank you.

…, this is …

Come and meet …

Hi, … How are you?

My name is …

Hello, …

Tipp
Auf die Frage „How are you?" wird im Englischen eine Kurzantwort wie „Fine" oder „Fine, thanks" erwartet.

B6 Come and meet my family

CD

Listen to the group of people.
How many people are there? What are their names?

C1 Boys have an easy life

Listen to the CD. Why are the girls angry?

CD

On Sunday Caroline and Gillian meet Charlie at the youth club.

Charlie: Hi Gillian, hi Caroline! Hey, Caroline, what's up?
Caroline: Oh, my brother George! He makes me so angry. He always plays tricks on me and he never helps at home – only on Saturdays.
Gillian: Boys have an easy life. They never do jobs at home.
Charlie: Never? I always feed my goldfish.
Gillian: It's your goldfish. And what about the washing up?
Charlie: Oh, sometimes. Well, um, I don't do the washing up.
Caroline: I always make my bed. And you?
Charlie: Well, my mum makes it but …
Gillian: And breakfast for your mum?
Charlie: Well, I often make tea for my mum on Sundays … and on Mothers' Day.
Caroline: Great! And the rubbish?
Charlie: Yuck! No, I don't take out the rubbish.
Caroline: You see? An easy life. I always take out the rubbish and I normally go shopping. You don't do the washing up. You don't take out the rubbish. George doesn't set the table and he never makes his bed. I think boys are lazy. What about you, Gillian?
Gillian: Well, I sometimes do the shopping. I normally water the plants. Oh, and I always clean the bathroom.
Charlie: OK, OK. You're right. But it's Sunday! Let's relax!
Caroline: Charlie Batson! An easy life!

LiF 14, 15

WB 17, 18

C2 Charlie never …

a) Talk about the friends' jobs.

Caroline Gillian Charlie	sometimes often normally never always	(water) (do) (make) (feed) (take out) (clean) (go)	the goldfish. the rubbish. shopping. the bathroom. breakfast. the bed. the washing up. the plants.

LiF -Ex 12, 14

Tipp
Nicht vergessen:
do – does
go – goes

b) Write about what Charlie does NOT do.
Charlie doesn't do the washing up. …

LiF-Ex 15

C3 Charlie, the big helper

LiF-Ex 14, 15

Look at the text in C1 again and say what is wrong.

Charlie says: "I have a hard life."
That's wrong. Charlie doesn't have a hard life ...

C4 What about you?

a) What do you always/normally/often/sometimes/never do at home? Make a grid.

	always	normally	often	sometimes	never
do the washing up	✓				
take out the rubbish					
clean the bathroom					
make my bed					
...					

LiF-Ex 12, 14, 15

WB 19

b) Talk about your jobs.

I always make my bed.

I never ...

Change grids with a partner. Talk about his/her jobs.

Lisa often does the washing up. She sometimes ...

extra

A cat's life

Write a short story.

always	*at 10 o'clock*
something	*at 12:30*
...	

C5 Classroom jobs

Who does what in your classroom?

WHO ...
... cleans the board?
... takes out the rubbish?
... waters the plants?
... collects the worksheets?
...?

Patrick always waters the plants.

Well, I tidy up the classroom on Mondays.

Milan and Johanna clean the board.

LiF-Ex 12

C6 Boys or girls?

a) Who says this – a boy or a girl?

I can use a computer.
I can't dance.
I'm good at maths.
I like fast cars.
I don't like drawing pictures.
I'm not good at basketball.
I can repair things.
I can cook.
I am strong.
I often go shopping.

I think a boy says sentence number 1.

Yes.

No.

I'm not sure.

b) Write the sentences on cards and hang them on the wall in your classroom. Look at the cards and tick the sentences that describe you. Boys take a red pencil and girls take a blue pencil.

project

"I can cook." Mmh .... Yes!

"I can't dance." No, that's not right!

c) Count the ticks for one sentence and tell the class about it.

Ten boys and twelve girls say they can use a computer.

Six girls and nine boys say they can cook.

C7 Charlie's week

On Mondays Charlie takes his sister Sharon to ballet school at four thirty. He doesn't like ballet. The next day Charlie goes to football training. After training he drinks lemonade and talks to his friends. Charlie is president of the Holland Park School Goldfish Club. He often writes articles for the magazine "Our Goldfish" on Wednesdays. Some people don't like his articles. Charlie doesn't like Thursdays. He has food technology in school and it is boring. On Fridays Charlie's parents go out so Charlie sometimes stays up late and plays computer games. On Saturday afternoons Charlie sometimes goes to an Arsenal match with his dad. The next morning Charlie makes his mum a cup of tea. Then he goes back to bed.

Match the pictures to the days.

WB 20

C8 The Batsons' plan

Look at the plan. Talk about the Batsons.

On Mondays and Wednesdays Sharon goes to ballet school.

	Sharon	Charlie	Josephine	Mum	Dad
MON	4:30-5:30 ballet school	4:30-5:30 ballet school (Sharon)			
TUE		4:00-5:30 football training	6:30-8:00 fitness club	11:00-2:00 school canteen	
WED	4:30-5:30 ballet school	3:30-4:30 Goldfish club		4:30-5:30 ballet school (Sharon)	
THU	3:30-4:30 school band			11:00-2:00 school canteen	
FRI		8:00-9:30 babysitting (Sharon)	6:00-7:30 fitness club	8:00-9:30 dancing class	8:00-9:30 dancing class
SAT					
SUN					

Tipp
In englischsprachigen Ländern wird die Uhrzeit oft anders angegeben. Schau auf Seite 151 nach.

choose

project

- **Draw pictures of your week and write about it. Look at C7 for help.**
- **Write a plan for your family and present it to the class. Look at C8 and in your dictionary for help.**

C9 Chain game

Write a job on a card. You can also draw and write about a hobby or a sport (play football, watch TV, ...).

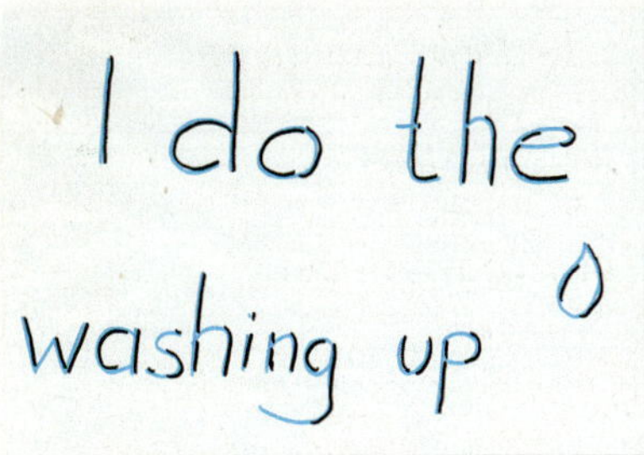

or

Play the game like this:

LiF-Ex 12

In diesem *Theme* hast du wieder einmal eine Menge gelernt – bravo!
Du kannst jetzt

- ✓ sagen, was sich in deinem Zimmer an welchem Platz befindet.
- ✓ mit Hilfe von Satzanfängen dein Zimmer beschreiben.
- ✓ über Alltagsaktivitäten, Aufgaben im Haushalt und Gewohnheiten sprechen und schreiben.
- ✓ über den Tagesablauf einer Person berichten.
- ✓ jemanden vorstellen.
- ✓ eine Geschichte anhand von Stichwörtern nacherzählen.

Das hast du super gemacht!

WE ARE SPRING-CLEANING

Music: James Delbridge, Arrangement: Jens Schliecker

CD

1. Listen to the song and sing along.
2. In groups of six act out the jobs you do at home and make up a dance. You can present the song at the next parents' night.

People I know

A1 School things

A2 Rajiv at school

How to ... read

Look at the pictures on this page.

- **What can you see?**
- **Who can you see?**
- **What day is it?**
- **Where are they?**
- **What time is it?**

What do you think the text in A3 is about?

A3 Rajiv's maths lesson

CD

It is Friday and Rajiv's last lesson is maths. His teacher Mr Graham is talking and his classmates are busy. Rajiv is not interested. He loves English and music, but numbers ... no, they are so boring.

Rajiv never listens to Mr Graham. In his lessons Rajiv sometimes dreams. Today he is dreaming about Caroline. In his dream they are dancing. Caroline is very nice. And she likes good music and dancing, too! It is fun to be with her. This Saturday they have an invitation to David's birthday party. David always has great music. Perhaps Rajiv can dance with Caroline. She dances very well. Rajiv smiles.

"Hey, Rajiv! Do you know the answer?", asks Mr Graham. Rajiv's face goes red.
"Err, no ... no sir, sorry ...". The bell rings. All the pupils jump up.
"Rajiv, you dream in class. I don't like that! Please listen to me in class!",
says Mr Graham when he is leaving the classroom.

WB 1

Look at the three parts of the text. How does Rajiv feel? What do you think?

I think Rajiv is happy in the blue part.

happy
bored
unhappy
friendly
funny
angry

A4 In the maths lesson

Find the words.

1. Mr Graham ___ Rajiv's maths teacher.
2. Rajiv ___ English and music.
3. Numbers ___ so boring.
4. Rajiv never ___ to Mr Graham.
5. David always ___ great music at his birthday party.
6. Caroline ___ very well.
7. Rajiv doesn't ___ the answer.
8. Rajiv's face ___ red.
9. The bell ___ and the pupils ___ up.

extra

Close your eyes and listen. Draw a picture of Rajiv's dream.

CD

A5 Rajiv's timetable

Tipp
Wenn du mehr über die Schule in Großbritannien erfahren möchtest, kannst du dir die Land & Leute-Box auf S. 77 anschauen.

Work with a partner. Look at Rajiv's timetable and talk about it.

NAME: Rajiv Khan — YEAR: 7c

		MONDAY	TUESDAY	WEDNESDAY	THURSDAY	FRIDAY
	8:40	Registration	/	Assembly		
1	9:00–9:40	English	Design and Technology	Geography	History	History
2	9:40–10:20	↓	↓	↓	Religious Education	Science
		Break				
3	10:40–11:20	Art	Science	English	Science	Physical Education
4	11:20–12:00	↓	French	Music	↓	↓
		Lunch				
		Registration				
5	1:20–2:00	Science	Information and Communication Technology	Maths	English	Music
6	2:00–2:40	Physical Education		French	Maths	Maths
7	2:40–3:20	↓	English	↓	Food Technology	↓

On Mondays Rajiv has … .

Rajiv's day always starts with … .
Rajiv has … lessons a week.

There are breaks at … and at … .
There is a/an … lesson on … .
There are two/three/… … lessons.

I think … is a very	interesting difficult easy nice boring …	subject.

WB 2, 3

A6 Timetable questions

a) **Match the parts and write down the questions.**

How long are	is the morning break?
How many English lessons	is lunch?
When	are there every week?
Is there a history lesson	lunch break?
What time	on Tuesday?
When is the	the lessons?

LiF-Ex 16

b) **How many questions can you answer?**

Here is some help:
How many …?
How long …?
When …?
What …?
Is there …?
Are there …?

extra

Work with a partner. Look at the timetable in A5. Can you ask more questions?

Land & Leute

SCHULALLTAG IN GROSSBRITANNIEN

Der Schulalltag dauert etwa von 9 bis 16 Uhr. In vielen Schulen trifft man sich als Erstes zur *registration*. Hier wird die Anwesenheit überprüft. Oft gibt es auch noch eine Schulversammlung, *assembly*, in der Ankündigungen gemacht werden, z. B. über Projektwochen, Sportveranstaltungen und Theateraufführungen. Danach beginnt dann der Unterricht.

In Großbritannien haben die Lehrerinnen und Lehrer eigene Unterrichtsräume. Die Schülerinnen und Schüler gehen also für jedes Fach in einen anderen Raum. In der Mittagspause kann man in der Kantine eine warme Mahlzeit essen. Vor oder nach dem Unterricht nehmen viele Schulkinder an Arbeitsgemeinschaften (*school clubs*) teil. Hier kann man Sport treiben, Musik machen, Schach spielen und vieles mehr.

Trotz ganztägigem Unterricht gibt es oft noch Hausaufgaben. Am Samstag ist überall schulfrei.

Hast du bemerkt, dass man an den meisten britischen Schulen eine Uniform trägt?

Kennst du den Schulalltag in anderen Ländern?

A7 Comparing timetables

a) Write down your timetable in English.

b) Compare Rajiv's timetable with your timetable.

Rajiv's day always starts with … .
    I don't have ... at my school.
On Monday Rajiv's first lesson is ... and starts at … .
    On Monday my first lesson is … and starts at … .
Rajiv has … lessons on Wednesday.
    I have … lessons on Wednesday.
Rajiv's lessons are … minutes.
    My lessons are … .
Rajiv's fourth lesson starts at … .
    My fourth lesson doesn't start at … .
    …

1st	**first**
2nd	**second**
3rd	**third**
4th	fourth
5th	**fifth**
6th	sixth
7th	seventh
8th	eig**hth**
9th	ni**nth**
10th	tenth

WB 4

A8 A quiz

CD

a) Listen to the CD. Which lessons can you hear?

b) Look at Rajiv's timetable in A5. Now listen again. What day is it?

A9 Morning song

Listen to the song.
Make four groups. Each group learns one verse by heart. Act out the verse.

WB 5-8

When do you get up every morning?
I get up at half past six.
When do you have your breakfast every morning?
I have my breakfast at six forty-five.
When do you clean your teeth every morning?
When do you dress and leave your house for school?
When do you ... What do you ... Where do you ... Why?
When do you dress and leave your house for school?

What do you have for breakfast every morning?
I have cornflakes, bacon, eggs and toast.
What do you drink for breakfast every morning?
I drink tea with a lot of milk.
What do you do when your breakfast is over?
What do you do before you leave your house?
When do you ... What do you ... Where do you ... Why?
What do you do before you leave your house?

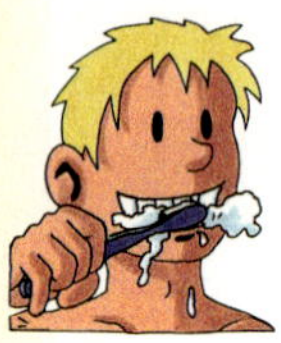

Where do you clean your teeth every morning?
I clean my teeth in our bathroom.
Where do you have your breakfast every morning?
I have my breakfast in the living room.
Where do you go when breakfast is over?
Where do you go when you leave your house?
When do you ... What do you ... Where do you ... Why?
Where do you go when you leave your house?

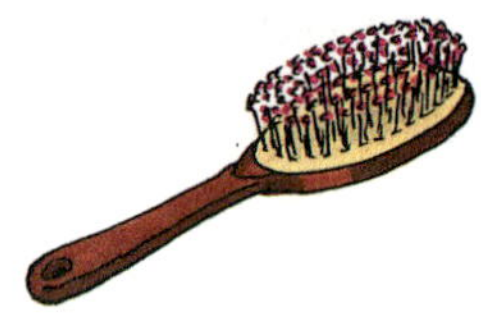

Why do you leave your house every morning?
I leave my house to walk to school.
Why do you take your schoolbag in the morning?
I have my homework safe inside.
Why do you clean your teeth in the morning?
Why do you brush your hair till it shines?
When do you ... What do you ... Where do you ... Why?
Why do you brush your hair till it shines?

© Text: Pat Jüngst

A10 When? What? Where? Why?

LiF-Ex 16

Write down all the questions in the song (verses 1, 2 and 3).

choose

- **What about your morning? Write down the answers.**
- **Work with a partner. Make an interview about his/her morning.**

11th eleven**th**
12th twel**fth**
13th thirteen**th**
14th fourteen**th**
15th fifteen**th**

16th sixteen**th**
17th seventeen**th**
18th eighteen**th**
19th nineteen**th**
20th twen**tieth**

21st twenty-**first**
22nd twenty-**second**
23rd twenty-**third**
24th twenty-four**th**
25th twenty-fi**fth**

26th twenty-six**th**
27th twenty-seven**th**
28th twenty-eigh**th**
29th twenty-nin**th**
30th thir**tieth**
31th thirty-first

B1 Birthday cards and invitations

This is David's invitation card to Rajiv. Make an invitation card for your birthday.

portfolio

WB 9-11

This is Emma's birthday card for David. Make a birthday card for your friend.

January
February
March
April
May
June
July
August
September
October
November
December

B2 Our birthdays

a) Ask your classmates:

When is your birthday?

It's in June.

It's on the second of March.

Tipp
Man schreibt: „2nd March."
Man sagt: „The second of March."

b) Make a birthday calendar for your class.

B3 Sound check

Can you say this?

CD

When is Aunt Ethel's birthday?
It's on Thursday.
It's on the thirtieth of May.
She will be thirty-three that day.
I'll go there with my brother,
With my father and my mother.
Aunt Ethel is my father's sister
That's the end of this tongue twister.

B4 A great present

A/An ... is a nice present for my friend.

What can you buy as a present for your friend?

–your mother
–your grandfather

CD

How to ... help out in English

B5 A birthday present

Rajiv needs a birthday present for David. He walks along Portobello Road. Perhaps he can get an idea at the market. Everyone is doing the shopping for the weekend. There are a lot of people and it is noisy. Mr Ram is busy at his fruit stall.

Rajiv walks past a clothes stall. Here you can buy T-shirts, caps, socks … . A T-shirt for David? Not really.

LiF 17, 18

Rajiv walks on. There are a lot of people. They want to buy potatoes, broccoli, carrots, cucumbers and more at the vegetable stall. Vegetables for a birthday? – No!

Then there is a poster stall. There are animal posters, football posters and posters of pop stars.
A poster for David? What does he like best? Rajiv is not sure and walks on.

Then Rajiv comes to a music stall. He looks at all the CDs, music videos and DVDs. – Yes, a CD! That's a fantastic present for David.

WB 12-15

Work with a partner. Read about the people at the market.
Are these sentences right or wrong?

1. Rajiv needs a Christmas present for David.
2. Mr Ram sells vegetables.
3. Mrs Roberts buys bananas.
4. The German girl wants to buy a blue T-shirt.
5. Rajiv buys tomatoes at the vegetable stall.
6. The man buys tomatoes and cucumbers.
7. You can buy posters of cats at the poster stall.
8. Rajiv buys a CD at the music stall.
9. David doesn't like hip hop.
10. Rajiv's change is £3.99.

B6 At the music stall

Look at Rajiv at the music stall.
Work with a partner. Find new words for the blue words. Act the scene.

B7 People at the market

a) Listen to the people at the market.
Can you find out where they are?

CD

b) Listen again. What do the people buy?

WB 16, 17

B8 A market day in your classroom

project

Have a market day in your classroom.

a) **What can you sell? Collect ideas:**
vegetables, CDs, posters, clothes …

b) **Make cards. Draw something you want to sell at the market. Write the name and the price on the back of the card.**

c) **Write shopping phrases on two cards. Make one card for the buyer and one card for the market seller. Then make shopping dialogues.**

Tipp
Das Verkaufsgespräch auf S. 41 kann dir helfen.

Right. Here you are!

Yes, can I have a/an/one/some … .

Excuse me.

Yes, I'd like one/two/three … .

Here's your change.

Thanks.

That's … .

Hello, can I help you?

How much is that/are they?

What can I do for you?

Here you are.

Thank you. Bye.

LiF-Ex 17

choose

- Work with a partner. Act your shopping dialogue in front of the class.
- Work with a partner. Record your dialogue.
- Make a market page for your portfolio.
  - You can write a shopping dialogue.
  - You can draw or stick a picture of a market on your page.
  - You can write a price list.

  Do you have more ideas for your market page?

portfolio

CD

C1 Party preparations

Today is David's birthday. It's two o'clock already so everyone is in a hurry. Grandma Williams is setting the table. David's father is preparing pizza, his mother and Aunt Fay are decorating the living room. Uncle Morgan is trying out the CD player. He is dancing and having a great time. David is taking photos with his new camera, a present from Aunt Fay.

LiF 19

Grandma Williams: David, watch out! Can't you see? I'm carrying glasses!
David: Say 'cheese', grandma.

David: Aunt Fay, look here!
Aunt Fay: Not now, David!
Mrs Williams: Morgan, can you help us, please? We're having problems with the decorations.
David: Smile, mum!
Aunt Fay: You and your uncle really are a big help!

Mr Williams: Stop that, David! I'm cutting the onions for your pizza.
David: Don't cry, dad. It's my birthday.

Look at the photos and say what everyone is doing.

WB 18

David
Uncle Morgan
Grandma Williams
David's mother and his Aunt Fay
David's father

is
are

crying.
decorating the living room.
carrying the glasses.
having problems with the decorations.
cutting the onions.
preparing pizza.
dancing.
having a great time.
taking photos.

LiF-Ex 19

C2 What a party!

CD

a) The party is fantastic! David and his guests are having a great time. What about Rajiv? Look at the photos and listen to the CD.

Tipp
Im Workbook kannst du die Fortsetzung finden.

b) Listen to the CD again and put the scenes in the correct order: *E, ...*

Look at the pictures again. What do you think happens next?

c) Work with a partner. Use these notes. Ask and answer like this:

WB 19-22

This person is blowing out the candles. Who is it?

That's David in picture B.

blowing out the candles
talking to Caroline
opening presents – saying hello
asking Caroline for a dance
playing a game

LiF-Ex 19

C3 Watch out!

a) Make lists like these:

eat	am/are/is **eating**

cut	am/are/is **cutting**

take	am/are/is **taking**

How to ... work with grammar

b) What do you notice? Find more examples in C1 and C2.

C4 Family tree

This is David's family tree.

a) When are the birthdays?

Gillian's birthday is on 15th January. …

WB 23, 24

b) Talk about David's family.

Gillian is David's cousin.
Morgan is David's uncle.
…

LiF-Ex 20

C5 Family tree quiz

Make a quiz for your partner.
Here are some ideas:

- Who is David's uncle?
- Is Alice Gillian's aunt?
- Whose first name starts with 'F'?
- How many brothers does Gwen have?
- Whose name has five letters?
- Whose birthday is on 13th September?
- …

daughter – son
grandmother – grandfather
mother – father
sister – brother
aunt – uncle
granddaughter – grandson
wife – husband
cousin – cousin
niece – nephew
parents – single parent
married – divorced

LiF-Ex 16

choose

- **Make a family tree of your family. Talk about it to a partner.**
- **Make a family tree of your fantasy family. Talk about it to a partner.**

portfolio

Du kannst jetzt schon …

✓ einen englischen Stundenplan lesen und über deinen Schulalltag sprechen.
✓ Fragen zum Thema Schule stellen.
✓ jemanden zum Geburtstag einladen und jemandem gratulieren.
✓ ein Verkaufsgespräch führen und dich beraten lassen.
✓ sagen, was jemand gerade tut.
✓ die Mitglieder einer Familie benennen.
✓ Wörter zu einem Thema nach Unterthemen ordnen.

Das ist schon ganz schön viel, oder? Du hast deine Sache sehr gut gemacht!

A brochure about your school

project

Plan it

- Think about **your** school.
  Write down all the words like this.

SCHOOL			
subjects	people	schoolbag	classroom
geography	teacher	pencil case	desk
sports	...	...	
...			

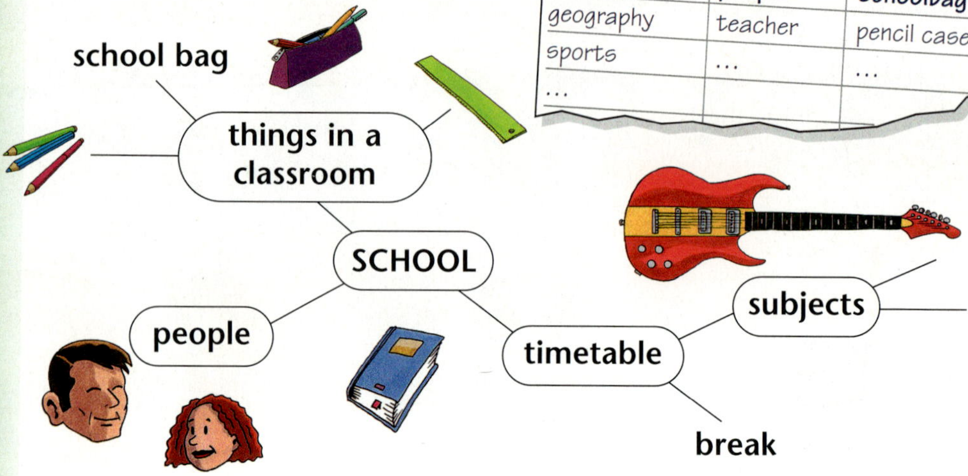

- Collect information about your school (How old is it? How many teachers are there? How many rooms are there? ...) Ask your teachers for help, too.

Do it

Make a brochure about your school. You need paper, colouring pencils and . Don't forget photos and pictures.

Check it

Are you happy with your brochure? Your teacher can help you with your English.

Present it

Hang it in the classroom.

6

Out and about

A1 What are you interested in?

> **Tipp**
> Wenn du noch ein paar Ideen benötigst, schau auf S. 44 nach.

computers

sport

I'm interested in … / I'm good at … .

animals

music

A2 Something for everyone

PROJECT WEEK AT HOLLAND PARK SCHOOL
JUNE 7th – JUNE 11th

A RAPPER'S DAY
– Song competition –

Write your own rap! Practise some moves for your song. Our members from the school band can help you.

Present your rap on stage.

B CATS KIDS CLUB
- Watch the great musical CATS.
- Learn to dance like a "cat"
- Meet some of the musical stars.
- Present your own CATS-show.

C LONDON PLANETARIUM

Are you interested in the stars and planets? Visit the planetarium. Watch the stars and learn about space.

Find out about your favourite planet and present your work.

D INLINE SKATING COMPETITION

Good at skating? Learn and practise some tricks.

Show what you can do and take part in the competition.

Read about the projects.

Which project are **you** interested in?

WB 1, 2

I like project B. Cats Kids Club sounds good to me.

I like … . … is a good project for me.

E OUTING TO KENTISH TOWN CITY FARM

Visit Kentish Town City Farm in Camden.
- See all the farm animals and feed them.
- Ride a tractor.
- Ride a pony, too.
- Milk a cow.

Write a report about your day on the farm.

F NEWSPAPER PROJECT

Want to be a reporter? Look at all the projects and interview pupils and teachers.

Write an article about the project week for the Holland Park School newspaper.

G DRAMA GROUP

So you want to be a big star? And you like detective stories? Then come to the drama group. Boys and girls welcome!

Act in our play **"A KNIFE IN THE BACK".**

H SIGHTSEEING TRIP: LONDON AQUARIUM

Visit the aquarium and find out about deep-sea animals. Watch your favourite animal and collect information about it.

Make your own "museum" in the classroom.

A3 What can they do?

Find projects for the pupils from Holland Park School. Look at the poster and talk about it.

... likes ...
... is ...
... has ...

Rajiv likes music and has a guitar. I think project A sounds good for him.

NAMES	INTERESTS
Janet	horses
Rajiv	music, guitar
Mary	sports, skateboard
Alice	theatre, detective stories
Charlie	music, president of Holland Park School Goldfish club
Kenny	computers, stories, photos
Will	Star Trek fan, telescope
Brenda	

A4 So many projects

Brenda doesn't know which project to take. So her teacher talks to her.

Listen to the CD and find out: Which project does Brenda choose?

CD

WB 3, 4

A5 Your favourites

What are your top three projects?

B1 Old McDonald …

Look at the picture of the farm.
Do you know the names of some of the animals?
- **Say the names of the animals.**
- **Work with a partner. Make a list of all the farm animals in English and German.**

CD

WB 5-8

LiF 21

B2 Farm information

The pupils asked a lot of questions at the farm information point. Look at their questions and find the right answers.

- Piglets? Yes, of course. They are over there – next to the barn and the trees.
- No, sorry, you can't.
- Go straight on. Then turn left and go over the bridge.
- There's a snack bar in the barn.
- Yes. Do you want one?

WB 9

B3 Sound check

Can you say this?

Three grey geese
in the green grass grazing.
Grey were the geese
and green was the grass.

CD

CD

B4 At the snack bar

a) Read the dialogue.

b) Look at the menu. Work with a partner and make new dialogues.

WB 10

B5 Hello from London

a) Read Janet's postcard.

b) Make a postcard for your home town.

portfolio

TIME-SAVING POSTCARD

Saying hello from London

Hello *Lilian*

The weather is *OK*.

Today it is rainy ☒ snowy ☐ cloudy ☒ windy ☐ sunny ☐ foggy ☐

Yesterday we visited

Tower Bridge ☐

Buckingham Palace ☐.

London Zoo ☐

Kentish Town City Farm ☒.

It was interesting ☒. boring ☐. OK ☐. fantastic ☐. terrible ☐.

Yours *Janet*

B6 A postcard to Caroline

It is still raining. There is a problem with Gillian's postcard to Caroline.

Can you still read it?

Dear Caroline,

Yesterday I ... at Kentish Town City Farm. It ... super. There ... cows, ponies, sheep and goats. And there ... ducks. There ... chickens and a cock next to the water.
My favourite animals ... the piglets. They always look so funny with their curly tails! But there ... a terrible smell so we ... only there for 5 minutes.
It ... an exciting day and I ... a lot of fun.

Bye for now. Yours, Gillian

Caroline Perrakis
28, West Avenue
London NW4

LiF-Ex 21

B7 The farm outing

Janet loved the farm outing. In the evening she talked to her parents about it.

There was/were ...
They had...
I/We looked at ...
It was ...

a tractor | 13 lambs | a bull | 4 ponies | interesting | a snack bar | goats | super | a barn | ...

LiF-Ex 21

WB 11-14

B8 Your outing to ...

Write about your last outing with your class. Use the beginnings of B7 for your text. Draw a picture.

portfolio

C1 What a week!

The newspaper group took some photos for the newspaper.

WB 15, 16

Match these notes with the photos.

LiF-Ex 21

a. These pupils had fun at the planetarium. There they looked at the stars.
b. There were big sharks at the London Aquarium.
c. Alice played the murderer in the play "A knife in the back".
d. Mary practised skating tricks for the competition.
e. These girls danced like cats at the musical theatre.
f. Brenda learned to milk a cow at Kentish Town City Farm.

Land & Leute

SCHOOL CLUBS

Nicht nur in der *project week* und während des *open day* gibt es viele Aktivitäten für die Schülerinnen und Schüler, sondern auch in den *school clubs*. An den meisten englischen Schulen können sich die Schülerinnen und Schüler in den Mittagspausen oder nach dem Unterricht in *school clubs* aufhalten. Das sind Arbeitsgemeinschaften, die oft mit Lehrern oder anderen Erwachsenen zusammenarbeiten.

Diese *school clubs* beschäftigen sich mit Hobbys und Sportarten, die auch bei uns bekannt sind. Theaterspielen, Chorsingen, Computerkurse, Karate, Fußball, Töpfern usw. Es gibt auch Schulclubs, die sich mit Dingen beschäftigen, die bei uns nicht so verbreitet sind: z. B. *gardening* oder Cricket.

C2 Farm talk

Find the right words.

1. Look at the cows. You can take a picture of them.
2. Look at the pig. I want to feed … .
3. I want to look at the ponies. Are you coming with … ?
4. There is a woman at the information point. Let's ask … where the toilets are.
5. Look at Brad. He is in the water. We must help … !
6. The piglets are so nice! I really like … .
7. The tractor is fun. I want to ride … .

him
it
them
me
her
…

LiF-Ex 13

C3 Newspaper project

This is Kenny's article about the farm outing.

a) **Read it. Do you like it?**

Cowgirls and bullfighters

Last Tuesday 10 pupils from Holland Park School visited Kentish Town City Farm in Camden. They looked at all the farm animals. There were cows, pigs, horses, goats, chicken and sheep. And there was a cock. Brenda learned to milk a cow. She had a lot of fun! Mr Graham, the teacher, liked his ride on the tractor. He talked to the farmer about the animals.

Poor Brad! A bull liked his red sweatshirt. It was an exciting day for everyone!

b) Nina was at the CATS kids club. This is her article.

Read Nina's article. What is wrong with it?

Miaow! Holland Park pupils visited CATS

18 boys and girls from Holland Park School visited CATS kids club this week.
[They] The boys and girls talked to the musical stars there. The musical stars played drama games with the pupils. That was very funny!
Bob learned to dance like a cat. Bob liked it very much.
Amy is good at art. Amy learned to do the CATS make-up. Mrs Simmons showed Amy some tricks.
At the end of the week the pupils had their own CATS show. The musical stars practised a song and CATS-dance with the pupils.
The pupils were superstars for one night!

WB 17, 18

LiF-Ex 13

c) **Kenny helped Nina. He underlined some words. Change these words. Is the article better now?**

she he they them they her

How to … write

C4 Open Day

a) Look at the poster. What is 'Open Day' about? Explain in one sentence.

How to ... read

WB 19, 20

Open Day at Holland Park School
Friday 11th July

HOLLAND PARK SCHOOL
The Royal Borough of Kensington and Chelsea

Rapper's Day
Listen to some great raps.
And come to our great song competition.
Room 132, 5:30 pm

Cats performance
Come and see this fantastic show.
Main Hall, 7:00 pm

Stars and planets: an exhibition
We collected interesting facts about planets like Mars and Jupiter and learned about the sun and the moon. Look at our posters and ask our experts about your favourite planet.
Look through our telescope.
Room 29, all afternoon

Inline skating competition
Watch fantastic tricks at the skating track.
Gym, 3:30-4:00 pm

Report on Kentish Town City Farm
Milking cows, riding a tractor, riding a horse, feeding goats ...
Farm life can be interesting. Find out what you can see at a city farm.
Take part in our bull-riding contest.
Room 37, 2:00-5:30 pm

"Underwater museum"
Visit our museum and "swim" like a fish.
Room 44, all afternoon

Holland Park School newspaper: special edition
Read all about the project week at Holland Park School.
Fascinating articles and great photos. You can get it at the school cafeteria for 50p.

We want to use the money for charity.

What a week!
Great interest in Holland Park School projects

Play: "A knife in the back"
So you like detective stories?
Then come and see our exciting play.
Main Hall, 8:00 pm

b) Look at the poster again. Make a list of the words you don't know. Look them up in the dictionary on pages 161-170.

c) Work with a partner. Compare your lists of words. Are they the same? Can you help your partner?

How to ... work with a dictionary

C5 A lot to see

WB 21

a) Look at the poster and find out the information. Make a list like this.

What's on?	Where?	When?

b) Talk to a partner.

What is your favourite show?

Where is it?

When is it?

C6 Fun at the Open Day

CD

Listen to the CD. Can you find out where the five pupils were?

I think the › first / second / third / ... › pupil › was at ... / watched ... / looked at ... / listened to ... / ... › ...

LiF-Ex 21

Du kannst jetzt schon ...

✓ über deine Interessen sprechen.
✓ etwas zum Essen und Trinken bestellen.
✓ über ein Ereignis aus der Vergangenheit berichten.
✓ Informationen von einem Plakat herauslesen.
✓ mit einem zweisprachigen Wörterbuch arbeiten.

Du hast in diesem *Theme* wieder ganz schön viel gelernt, bravo!

Have a great holiday!

A knife in the back

(Scene: The library in an old house. A man sits at a desk, sleeping. Enter the butler.)

Butler: Oh, Dr Goldman, here's your tea!

(He puts the tea on the table and goes out. Enter old Mrs Thorn, the cook. She can't hear very well.)

Mrs Thorn: Dr Goldman! I can't find my bike. I want to go to the shops but my bike isn't there. Where is my bike, Mr Goldman? Oh dear! He never knows a thing!

(Exit Mrs Thorn. Enter Jack Goldman, Dr Goldman's son.)

Jack: Hello, Dad. Can you give me some money? Five pounds? I want to go to the cinema. Dad? Always sleeping! Oh, well!

(Jack goes out, angry. Enter Jill Goldman, Dr Goldman's daughter.)

Jill: Oh, Daddy! Wonderful news. I'm the winner of the school reading competition.

(She runs to her father. He falls onto the table. There is a knife in his back.)

Jill: Aaargh!

(Enter Detective Blake.)

Detective Blake: Calm down, Jill. Let me see your father. Dr Goldman! Dr Goldman! Oh no, he's dead. We must call the police.

Jill: But you are a detective. Can't you find out who killed him?

Detective Blake: OK. First I must see all the people who were in the house. Can you bring them here?

(Jill goes out. Enter Mrs Thorn, Jack, the butler, and Jill.)

Detective Blake: Right. Sit down everyone. Now then … I must ask you all some questions …

(Scene: All the people in the house are in the library.)

Detective Blake: … well, this is very difficult. Let me think …
Dr Goldman had lunch and then he worked in the library.
He was killed in the afternoon. He was already dead when Mrs Thorn asked about her bike. And he was already dead when Jack asked him for some money. Jill is a nice girl. She loved her father. And she was at school when it happened. She is the winner of the reading competition.
But what about you, sir? You are the butler at the Goldmans.
You were alone with him in the library.
I know that Dr Goldman wanted you to leave the family because you aren't a good butler. He wanted a new butler. So you hated him – and you killed him.

(Everyone looks at the butler, their mouths open.)

Butler: … Detective Blake, you're right. I hated him. I killed him because I wanted to keep my job with the family – this is the only thing I've got. This is my life.

(The butler is crying.)

Detective Blake: Come on, let's go to the police.

(Detective Blake and the butler go out. The curtain falls.)

choose

- **Draw the scenes.**

- **Work in groups of six and act out the play.**

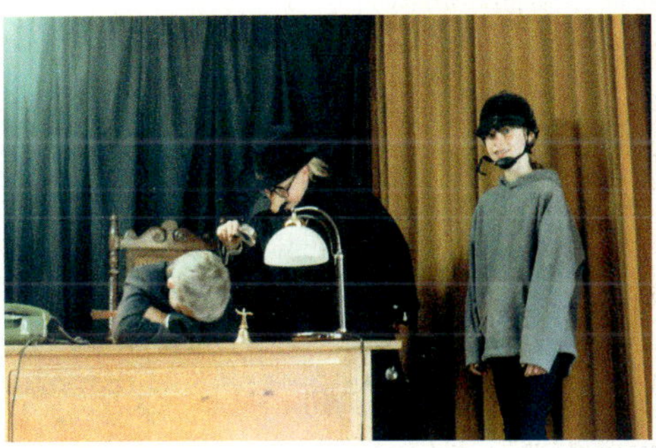

Do you want a pen pal? No problem! Try www.penpalworld.com.
You can tell your new pen pal about your family, your hobbies, your school, your favourite animal/pop group/movie … .

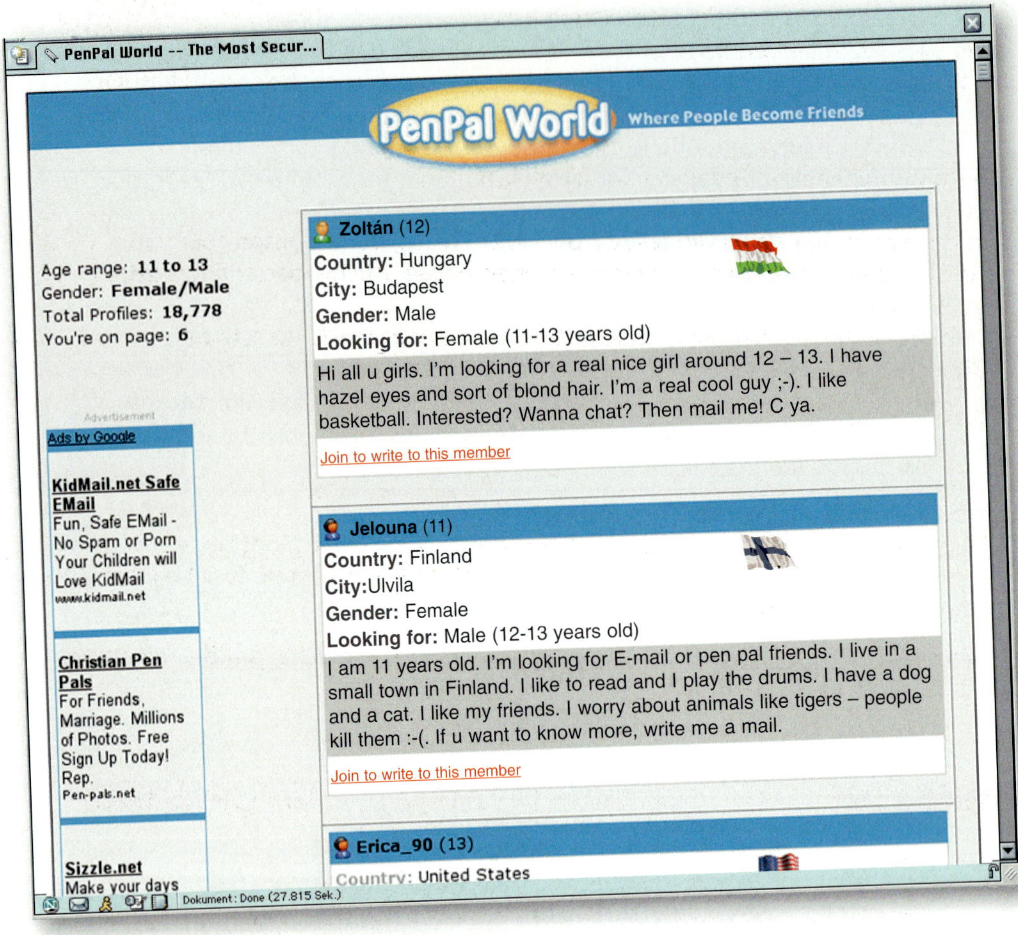

Useful lists:

e-mail language:

R – are
C – see
B – be
U – you
4 – for
2 – too

emoticons:

:-)	happy
:-(	sad
;-)	joking
:-o	shocked
:-x	kiss
:'-(	crying
((Name))	hug
(( )):**	hugs and kisses

Can you read these?

ICU. RUOK? B nice. Good 4 U.

Ohren auf! – Worum geht es überhaupt?

Im Unterricht hörst du oft Geschichten und Gespräche auf Englisch. Es ist nicht so einfach, immer alles sofort zu verstehen.
Hier sind einige Tipps, die dir helfen können:

A Before you listen – Bevor du ein Gespräch oder eine Geschichte anhörst:
In deinem Englischbuch findest du oft Bilder zu englischen Gesprächen oder Geschichten. Sie können dir beim Verstehen helfen. Auch Überschriften geben dir gute Hinweise.
Sieh dir die Bilder und die Überschrift genau an. Was weißt du schon?
Überlege: Worum könnte es wohl gehen?

Was erwartest du?

B Now listen – Beim Hören:
Höre dir das Gespräch oder die Geschichte einmal ganz an. Dabei ist es nicht so wichtig, dass du jedes einzelne Wort verstehst. Vielleicht hast du ja schon eine Idee, worum es gehen könnte.

Wenn das Gespräch oder die Geschichte zu Ende ist, versuche, auf die folgenden Fragen Antworten zu finden:

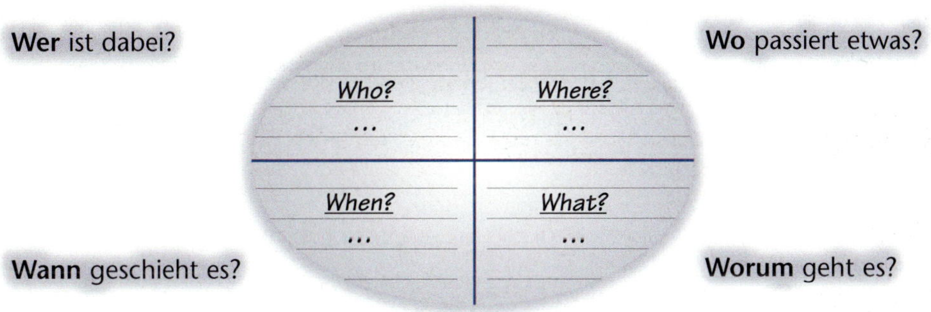

Listen again: Höre dir das Gespräch/die Geschichte noch einmal an.

Mache dir Notizen zu den Fragen. Manche Felder werden vielleicht leer bleiben.

C Last but not least – Zu guter Letzt
Vergleiche deine Ergebnisse mit einem/r Partner/in. Was habt ihr herausgefunden? Haben sich eure Erwartungen bestätigt?

Wie du Wörter notieren kannst

Klar, du kannst nicht Englisch sprechen, ohne dass du englische Wörter kennst! Aber wie bekommst du sie in deinen Kopf? Erstmal solltest du sie notieren. Hier sind einige Möglichkeiten:

- Sammle Wörter, die zu einem Oberbegriff passen, in einer Tabelle.

FOOD	DRINKS	SCHOOL	PEOPLE
ice cream	milk	pen	friend
apple	coke	board	sister
...	...	...	...

- Du kannst auch ein Gedankennetz (*mindmap*) anfertigen. Dabei verbindest du alle Wörter miteinander, die zu einem Thema passen.

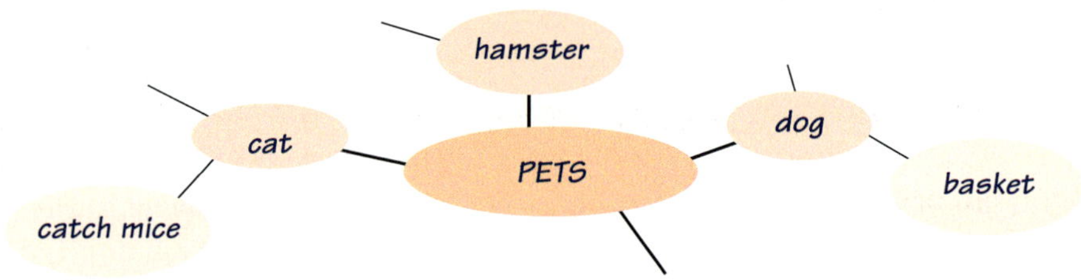

- Du kannst auch einfache Listen erstellen. Zum Beispiel eine Liste für Wörter, die dir Schwierigkeiten bereiten. Oder eine Liste mit deinen Lieblingswörtern. Und natürlich deine persönliche Wortliste!

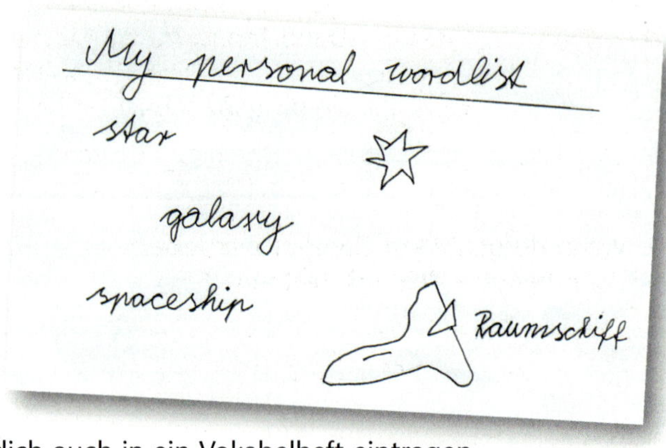

- Du kannst englische Wörter natürlich auch in ein Vokabelheft eintragen.

Last but not least – Zu guter Letzt
Wie wäre es, wenn du dir einen Hefter anlegst? Dort kannst du deine Wortsammlungen und Listen einheften und immer wieder mit neuen Seiten ergänzen.

Wie du Wörter behalten kannst

Du hast sicher schon viele Wörter notiert. Nun kommt es darauf an, dass du sie auch behältst! Hier sind einige Tipps, die dir dabei helfen.

- Bist du ein „Bildertyp“? Dann kannst du aus Wörtern Bilder machen oder die Wörter durch eigene Bilder ergänzen.

- Knobelst du gerne? Dann versuche doch mal, mit den Wörtern, die du dir merken willst, Sätze zu bauen. Sie können ruhig lustig sein – um so besser kannst du dir die Wörter merken.

  My football is in the freezer.

- Bist du eher ein „Hingucker“? Dann schreibe die Wörter auf Klebezettel. Hänge sie zu Hause an verschiedenen Stellen auf, dann hast du sie immer im Blick.

- Vielleicht bist du ja auch ein guter Zuhörer. Dann kannst du die Wörter aufnehmen und sie dir immer wieder anhören. So prägst du sie dir ganz schnell ein!

- Wenn du gerne am Computer arbeitest, dann benutze den Vokabeltrainer!

- Bist du ein Blitzmerker? Wenn du gut auswendig lernen kannst, kannst du dir 10-15 Wörter immer wieder aufsagen. So lernst du sie auch ganz schnell.

Grammatikregeln auf der Spur

Grammatikregeln können helfen, dein Englisch zu verbessern. Du findest sie im LiF-Teil deines Englischbuches. Grammatik muss aber nicht langweilig sein! Spiele Detektiv und versuche, Grammatikregeln selbst auszutüfteln. Das macht großen Spaß und geht so:

1. Sammle mehrere Beispiele, die ähnlich aussehen.

2. Sortiere: Schreibe die Beispiele untereinander. Was sieht hier ähnlich aus? Unterstreiche die Stellen.

one hand	*eight hands*
my toe	*ten toes*
a hand	*two hands*

oder

have	*am/is/are*	*having*
dance	*am/is/are*	*dancing*
take	*am/is/are*	*taking*

3. Sieh dir deine Beispiele gut an. Was kannst du erkennen? Versuche zu beschreiben, welche Veränderung immer wieder auftritt.

Wenn ein englisches Wort in der Mehrzahl steht, dann wird ein -s angehängt.

oder

Endet ein Verb im Infinitiv auf -e, so fällt das e bei der ing-Form weg.

Bravo! Schon hast du deine ersten Grammatikregeln aufgespürt!

Last but not least – Zu guter Letzt
Manchmal gibt es auch eine Ausnahme, die nicht zu einer Grammatikregel passt. Zum Beispiel:

one foot	*eight feet*
a mouse	*ten mice*

Diese Beispiele musst du dir dann noch einmal extra gut einprägen. Aber keine Sorge: So viele Ausnahmen gibt es im Englischen nun auch wieder nicht!

Lesen leicht gemacht!

Im Englischunterricht begegnen dir ganz viele englische Geschichten, Zeitungsartikel, Gedichte … . Sicher willst du genau wissen, worum es da geht. Auf den ersten Blick sieht das vielleicht schwierig aus. Aber kein Problem – hier sind einige Tipps und Kniffe für dich:

A Before you read – Bevor du liest

Zu Geschichten, Zeitungsartikeln, Gedichten usw. gehören oft Bilder. Sie können dir beim Verstehen helfen. Auch Überschriften geben dir gute Hinweise.
Sieh dir die Bilder und die Überschrift genau an. Was weißt du schon? Überlege:
Worum könnte es wohl gehen?
Was erwartest du?

B Now read – Beim Lesen

Überfliege den Lesetext erst einmal. Dabei ist es nicht so wichtig, dass du jedes einzelne Wort verstehst. Vielleicht hast du ja schon eine Idee, worum es gehen könnte.

Versuche, auf die folgenden Fragen Antworten zu finden:

Wer ist dabei?

Wo passiert etwas?

Wann geschieht es?

Worum geht es?

Read again – Lies noch einmal.

Mache dir Notizen zu den Fragen. Manche Felder werden vielleicht leer bleiben.

C Last but not least – Zu guter Letzt

Zum Schluss kannst du deine Ergebnisse mit einem/r Partner/in vergleichen. Was habt ihr herausgefunden? Haben sich eure Erwartungen bestätigt?

Tipp Tipp Tipp Tipp:

Bevor du gleich Wörter im Wörterbuch nachschlägst, solltest du folgende Schritte versuchen, um die Bedeutung eines Wortes ohne Wörterbuch herauszufinden:

sports centre – information – crocodile
Kennst du vielleicht ein ähnlich klingendes deutsches Wort? Es wird dir sicherlich nicht schwer fallen, die Bedeutung zu erraten.

Charlie, the big helper
Kennst du vielleicht ein ähnliches englisches Wort? Denk an *help*. Was könnte *helper* heißen?

Versuche ein Wort aus dem gesamten Satz heraus zu verstehen. Hier ein Beispiel:
Das Wort ‚bloppy' gibt es nicht. Was könnte es im folgenden Satz bedeuten?
I always have cornflakes with 'bloppy' for breakfast.

Du kannst reden!

Reden kannst du ja bestimmt ganz gut, oder? Aber kannst du auch auf Englisch Gespräche führen? Das ist manchmal gar nicht so einfach. Nur keine Angst – hier findest du einige Tricks und Kniffe, um dich gut auszudrücken.

A Before you talk – Bevor du ein Gespräch führst

Überlege:
Wo befindest du dich?
Was möchtest du sagen?
Mit wem möchtest du sprechen?
Wie kannst du etwas höflich sagen oder fragen?

Sammle deine Gedanken.

B Now talk – Beim Reden

In einem Gespräch geht es darum, sich mit jemandem auszutauschen. Deshalb ist es wichtig, das Gespräch am Laufen zu halten. Mache zustimmende Geräusche und Bewegungen – z. B. nicke, wenn du etwas verstehst.

Du musst nicht jedes Wort verstehen. Achte auf deine/n Gesprächspartner/in. Am Gesichtsausdruck oder an Bewegungen kann man oft schon gut erkennen, worum es ungefähr geht. Auch der Tonfall deines/r Partners/in gibt dir Hinweise.

C Last but not least – Zu guter Letzt

Wenn du merkst, dass du etwas nicht ganz verstehst, dann …

… frage nach: *Sorry, what was that again?*

… bitte deinen Gesprächspartner, sich zu wiederholen: *Sorry, can you say that again, please?*

… überbrücke Gedankenpausen: *Well, … Hmm, …*

Schreiben macht Spaß!

Texte schreiben funktioniert im Englischen genauso wie im Deutschen.
Sicher möchtest du nun auch einmal etwas schreiben, oder? Na, dann los!

A Before you write – Bevor du schreibst
Damit du genug Wörter zu einem Thema hast, sammle Stichwörter für deinen Text.
Du kannst hierzu ein Gedankennetz – *mindmap* – oder eine Liste erstellen.

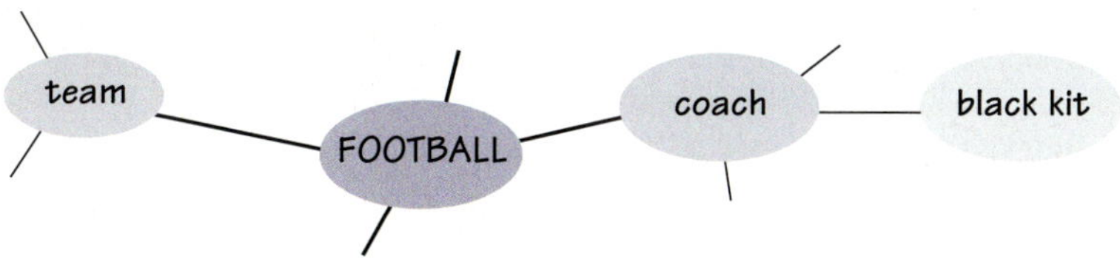

Tipp
Auf S. 102 kannst du sehen, wie das geht.

B Now write – Beim Schreiben
Wenn du eine Geschichte, ein Gedicht usw. schreiben möchtest, dann schreibe erst einmal kurze, einfache Sätze auf.

Oder:

Sieh dir die E-Mails und Berichte der *Portobello Road Kids* an.
Du kannst sie als Muster benutzen, um deine eigenen Texte zu schreiben.
Ersetze die Wörter, die nicht zu dir passen – und schon hast du etwas Eigenes über dich geschrieben!

Überlege dir nun eine Überschrift.
Sieh dir alles noch einmal an. Kannst du noch etwas verbessern?

C Last but not least – Zu guter Letzt
Gib deinen Text einer Mitschülerin/einem Mitschüler und lies ihren/seinen.
Was hast du erfahren? Sprecht über eure Texte. Passen die Überschriften noch?

Tipp
Du kannst deine Ergebnisse in deinem Portfolio abheften.

Noch ein paar Tipps und Tricks:

Tipp Tipp Tipp:

Hast du alles richtig geschrieben? Suchst du die Übersetzung für ein deutsches Wort? Gucke einfach ganz hinten im *dictionary* ab S. 173 nach.

Fange nicht jeden Satz gleich an.
Robert is my friend. Robert is eleven. → *Robert is my friend. He is eleven.*

Verbinde zwei Sätze mit *and*.
My cat Susie is black. She has green eyes. → *My cat Susie is black and has green eyes.*

Bist du bei der Grammatik unsicher? Schau im LiF-Teil ab S. 111 nach!

How to work with a dictionary

Ganz schnell Wörter finden

Du kannst nicht von jedem deutschen Wort wissen, was es auf Englisch heißt. Aber: Du kannst lernen, wo du es findest! Und das geht so:

A In deinem Englischbuch befindet sich ganz am Ende ein *dictionary.* Das ist ein Wörterbuch. Dort findest du alle Wörter, die in diesem Buch vorkommen.

Wenn du ein englisches Wort nicht verstehst, kannst du es im English-German *dictionary* ab S. 163 nachschlagen.

Wenn du etwas auf Englisch sagen willst und du ein Wort brauchst, das du nicht kennst, kann dir das German-English *dictionary* ab S. 173 helfen.

B Sieh dabei gut hin: Die Wörter sind alphabetisch geordnet. Du musst nicht nur auf den ersten Buchstaben achten, sondern auch auf den zweiten oder sogar dritten. Das Wort *cage* steht zum Beispiel vor *cake.*

Tipp
Das englische Alphabet findest du auf S. 123.

C

cage [keɪdʒ] Käfig 3/C4
cake [keɪk] Kuchen 1/A5
°cake pan ['keɪk ˌpæn] Kuchenform 2/B6
calendar ['kæləndə] Kalen-

C Es gibt oft mehrere Bedeutungen für ein Wort. Schau dir also den ganzen Abschnitt genau an, damit du die richtige Übersetzung findest.

Sieh dir die folgenden Sätze an. Welche Bedeutungen hat das Wort **clean** hier?

Tipp
Mehr Hinweise zum *dictionary* findest du auf S. 122.

I always clean my bedroom on Fridays.
Charlie's bedroom is always clean.

classroom ['klɑːsˌruːm] Klassenzimmer 1/A7
clean [kliːn] sauber machen; putzen 4/B1
°clean [kliːn] sauber 3/O3
clear [klɪə] klar; aufgeräumt 4/A5

Je öfter du Wörter im *dictionary* nachschlägst, um so schneller findest du sie. Du bist bestimmt schon bald ein richtiger Nachschlage-Profi!

Dolmetschen für Profis!

Du kannst jetzt schon gut Englisch verstehen und auch besser sprechen als manch andere/r. Das wird ein großer Vorteil sein, wenn du einmal mit Personen unterwegs bist, die kaum Englisch sprechen. Denen kannst du dann nämlich helfen! Das ist gar nicht so schwierig.

Jemandem in Englisch auszuhelfen, heißt nicht, wörtlich zu übersetzen! Du musst nicht jedes Wort verstehen, um jemandem mitzuteilen, was gemeint ist.

Stell dir vor, du bist mit deinen Eltern in London. Es ist Montag und ihr möchtet euch die *Kentish Town City Farm* ansehen. Da du verstehen kannst, was auf dem Schild steht, kannst du deinen Eltern sagen, dass die Farm montags geschlossen ist und ihr am nächsten Tag wiederkommen müsst!

oder

Es kann dir passieren, dass du in deiner Stadt beim Bäcker bist und hörst, wie jemand auf Englisch fünf Brötchen bestellt. Vielleicht versteht die Verkäuferin kein Englisch. Du kannst hier aushelfen! Du kannst der Verkäuferin sagen, was die Person gerne hätte und du kannst der Person den Preis auf Englisch nennen. Etwa so:

Classroom phrases

Wenn man ankommt oder geht

Good morning.	Guten Morgen.
Sorry, I'm late.	Tut mir Leid, dass ich zu spät komme.
Sorry, I don't have my exercise book with me.	Tut mir Leid, ich habe mein Heft nicht dabei.
Sorry, I don't have my homework with me.	Tut mir Leid, ich habe meine Hausaufgaben nicht dabei.
What's for homework?	Was haben wir als Hausaufgabe auf?
See you tomorrow.	Bis morgen.

Wenn es ein Problem gibt

What's the matter with you?	Was ist mit dir los?
I'm fine./I feel sick.	Mir geht's gut./Mir ist schlecht.
I have a headache.	Ich habe Kopfschmerzen.
Can I open the window, please?	Kann ich bitte das Fenster öffnen?
Can I go to the toilet, please?	Kann ich bitte zur Toilette gehen?

Wenn man Hilfe braucht

Can you help me, please?	Können Sie/Kannst du mir bitte helfen?
I have a question.	Ich habe eine Frage.
I don't understand this.	Ich verstehe das hier nicht.
How can I do this exercise?	Wie mache ich diese Aufgabe?
What's … in English/German?	Was heißt … auf Englisch/Deutsch?
What does … mean?	Was bedeutet …?
Can you write it on the board, please?	Können Sie/Kannst du das bitte an die Tafel schreiben?
Can you say that again, please?	Können Sie/Kannst du das bitte noch einmal sagen?
Sorry, I don't know.	Tut mir leid, das weiß ich nicht.
What page, please?	Auf welcher Seite bitte?

Wenn man zusammen arbeitet oder spielt

Whose turn is it?	Wer ist dran?
I (don't) like this story.	Diese Geschichte gefällt mir (nicht).
I think it's good/interesting/funny.	Ich finde sie gut/interessant/komisch.
I think it's terrible/boring/sad.	Ich finde sie schrecklich/langweilig/traurig.
Do you want to work with me?	Möchtest du mit mir arbeiten?

Was die Lehrerin oder der Lehrer sagt

Open your books at page …	Öffnet eure Bücher auf Seite …
Turn to page …	Blättert zu Seite …
Come to the board, please.	Komm/Kommt bitte zur Tafel.
Collect the exercise books, please.	Sammelt bitte die Hefte ein.
Do this exercise at home, please.	Macht diese Aufgabe bitte zu Hause.
Be quiet.	Sei ruhig./Seid ruhig.
Sit down.	Setz dich./Setzt euch.
Please speak up.	Sprich bitte lauter.
You can do better.	Das kannst du besser.
Try again.	Versuch es noch einmal.
That's it.	Das ist alles.
Well done.	Gut gemacht.

Im Abschnitt **Language in Focus** (LiF) wird die englische Sprache ganz genau unter die Lupe genommen. Sherlock Bear hilft dir dabei.

Immer, wenn du dieses Symbol vorne in deinem Buch siehst, kannst du in diesem Abschnitt nachsehen, welche Regeln es in der englischen Sprache gibt. Sherlock Bear gibt dir wichtige Hinweise und Tipps zu Grammatik.
Um dir die Regeln besser einzuprägen, kannst du sie noch einmal in dein eigenes Grammatikheft schreiben. Dort kannst du sie in deinen eigenen Worten notieren und weitere Beispielsätze finden.

Wenn du dieses Symbol vorne im Buch siehst, wird etwas geübt, was du bereits kennst. Wenn du dich unsicher fühlst, kannst du hier nochmal nachsehen.

1 Persönliche Fürwörter (Personalpronomen)

Mit dem Personalpronomen kann man etwas über sich oder andere Personen sagen.

- **I** wird immer groß geschrieben, auch wenn es mitten im Satz vorkommt.
- **you** benutzt man, wenn man jemanden anspricht. Es kann sowohl *du* als auch *Sie* oder *ihr* heißen.
- **he** und **she** beziehen sich auf Menschen und Haustiere, die einen Namen haben.
- **it** benutzt man für Gegenstände und andere Lebewesen (Tiere, Pflanzen, usw.)

I	*ich*
you	*du/Sie*
he	*er*
she	*sie*
it	*es*
we	*wir*
you	*ihr/Sie*
they	*sie*

2 Formen von ,be'

- **be** heißt auf Deutsch *sein*. Die Formen von **be** heißen *am, is* und *are.*
- Beim Sprechen benutzt man die **Kurzform**, beim Schreiben häufig die **Langform**.

Langform	Kurzform	
I am	I'm	*ich bin*
you are	you're	*du bist, Sie sind*
he is	he's	*er ist*
she is	she's	*sie ist*
it is	it's	*es ist*
we are	we're	*wir sind*
you are	you're	*ihr seid, Sie sind*
they are	they're	*sie sind*

- Übrigens:
  Wenn man das Verb **be** in der Verneinung benutzt, wird an die entsprechende Form **not** angehängt. Auch hier gibt es Lang- und Kurzformen:

Langform	Kurzform	
I am not	I'm not	*ich bin nicht*
you are not	you aren't	*du bist nicht, Sie sind nicht*
he is not	he isn't	*er ist nicht*
she is not	she isn't	*sie ist nicht*
it is not	it isn't	*es ist nicht*
we are not	we aren't	*wir sind nicht*
you are not	you aren't	*ihr seid nicht, Sie sind nicht*
they are not	they aren't	*sie sind nicht*

- Die Kurzform von **is** wird häufig auch nach anderen Wörtern benutzt: *what's, who's, there's, that's.*

3 Die Artikel

- Im Englischen gibt es nur eine Form des bestimmten Artikels: **the** (*der, die, das*).

  the market *der Markt*
  the cat *die Katze*
  the house *das Haus*
  the friends *die Freunde*

- Der unbestimmte Artikel (*ein/eine*) heißt **a** oder **an**.
  Vor Vokalen (*a, e, i, o* und bis auf wenige Ausnahmen vor *u*) steht **an** statt **a**:
  Es heißt:

  a ruler *aber* **an** exercise book
  a red apple *aber* **an** apple
  a T-shirt *aber* **an** orange T-shirt

4 there is .../there are ...

Wenn eine Sache oder eine Person vorhanden ist, sagt man **there is**, bei mehreren Sachen oder Personen sagt man **there are**.

There is a snack bar in Notting Hill.
Es gibt einen Schnellimbiss in Notting Hill.
In Notting Hill ist ein Schnellimbiss.

There are a lot of stalls at a street market.
Es gibt viele Stände auf einem Straßenmarkt.
Auf einem Straßenmarkt sind viele Stände.

5 Besitzanzeigende Fürwörter (Possessivpronomen)

- Mit den Possessivpronomen kann man sagen, wem etwas gehört oder zu wem jemand gehört.

my	*mein/e*
your	*dein/e, Ihr/e*
his	*sein/e*
her	*ihr/e*
its	*sein/e*
our	*unser/e*
your	*euer/eure, Ihr/e*
their	*ihr/e*

- **its** benutzt man bei Dingen und bei Tieren, deren Namen nicht bekannt sind.

The dog is in **its** house.

6 Pluralbildung (Mehrzahl)

- Von Hauptwörtern (Substantiven) bildet man die Mehrzahl (den Plural), indem man einfach ein **-s** anhängt:
  1 bike (*Fahrrad*) ➔ 2 bike**s** (*Fahrräder*)
  1 pencil (*Bleistift*) ➔ pencil**s** (*Bleistifte*)

- Wörter, die mit einem Zischlaut oder einem **-s** enden, erhalten in der Mehrzahl ein **-es**:
  1 class ➔ 2 class**es**
  1 sandwiches ➔ sandwich**es**
  1 box ➔ 2 box**es**

- Es gibt auch Hauptwörter, die die Mehrzahl nicht mit **-s** bilden. Diese unregelmäßigen Pluralformen sollte man immer zusammen mit der Einzahlform (Singular) lernen. Sie stehen in der Vokabelliste ab Seite 124 immer hinter dem Wort. Sieh doch einmal bei diesen Wörtern nach: *woman, mouse.* Du kannst auch schon mal bei LiF 17 nachschauen.

one man

two men

eight feet

one foot

7 Fragen und Kurzantworten

- Im Englischen antwortet man auf Fragen, die man mit ja oder nein beantworten kann, nicht nur *yes* oder *no.* Das klingt etwas unhöflich. Deshalb fügt man eine zusätzliche Bestätigung oder Ablehnung hinzu: **Yes, it is./No, it isn't.**
- In bejahenden Antworten kann man die Kurzform (z. B. *you're*) nicht verwenden, in verneinenden Antworten schon.

Frage	bejahende Antwort	verneinende Antwort
Is Caroline from Hendon?	Yes, she is.	No, she isn't.
Is Charlie from Hendon, too?	Yes, he is.	No, he isn't.
Is the butter on the table?	Yes, it is.	No, it isn't.
Are we all ready?	Yes, we are.	No, we aren't.
Are her eyes blue?	Yes, they are.	No, they aren't.

8 Präpositionen

Um zu sagen, wo sich etwas befindet, benutzt man Präpositionen (Verhältniswörter).

9 can/can't

- Mit dem Hilfsverb **can** sagt man, was jemand tun kann, mit **can't**, was man nicht tun kann oder darf.
  Can und **can't** wird für alle Personen benutzt.

Ich kann schnell laufen.

Du darfst jetzt kein Eis essen, aber du darfst einen Apfel essen.

- Auch Fragen und Antworten mit **can** und **can't** werden immer mit derselben Form gebildet.

10 have/has

Mit dem Verb **have** kann man ausdrücken, was man hat.
In der dritten Person Einzahl (also bei *he, she, it* oder bei Namen, für die man *he, she, it* einsetzen kann) benutzt man **has**.

I	have	a lot of CDs.	*ich habe*
You	have	a nice school scarf.	*du hast/Sie haben*
Mary	has	a cold.	*sie hat*
He	has	blue eyes.	*er hat*
The cat	has	white feet.	*es hat*
We	have	a great girls' team.	*wir haben*
You	have	red T-shirts.	*ihr habt*
They	have	a football match on Saturdays.	*sie haben*

11 Satzstellung

Der Bauplan einfacher englischer Sätze sieht so aus:

Subjekt *wer*	**Verb** *tut*	**Objekt** *was*	*(mit wem, wo, wann, usw.)*
I	play	football	with my friends. in the park. in the afternoon.

12 Die einfache Gegenwart (simple present)

- Die einfache Gegenwart benutzt man, wenn man über Gewohnheiten oder regelmäßig vorkommende Ereignisse spricht. Man benutzt sie auch, wenn man beschreibt, dass jemand mehrere Dinge nacheinander tut (z. B. in einer Geschichte).
- Genau wie im Deutschen haben die Verben im Englischen nicht für alle Personen die gleiche Endung. (Man sagt, *ich gehe*, aber *er geh***t** und *wir geh***en**.) Im Englischen braucht man sich nur zwei Formen zu merken.
- Das **simple present** hat dieselbe Form wie der Infinitiv, z. B. *play*. Nur in der 3. Person Einzahl (*he–she–it*) wird einfach ein **-s** angehängt.

I	play	football.
You	play	tennis.
He	play**s**	cricket.
She	play**s**	hockey.
It	play**s**	with a ball.
We	play	basketball.
You	play	cards.
They	play	games.

- Endet das Verb mit einem Zischlaut oder einem **-s**, muss bei *he, she, it* ein **-es** angehängt werden.

You	normally wash	your face.
He	normally wash**es**	his face.
We	often watch	TV.
She	often watch**es**	TV.

- Aufgepasst! Einige Verben haben eine besondere Schreibweise:

I	do	the cooking.
He	do**es**	the cooking.
We	go	to the football match.
She	go**es**	to the football match.
They	tidy	their room.
He	tid**ies**	his room.

13 Personalpronomen als Objekt

Im Deutschen gibt es den *Wem*-Fall (Dativ) und den *Wen*-Fall (Akkusativ).
Im Englischen gibt es nur eine Objektform:

Emma kann ihr helfen. (wem?)	Emma can help **her**.
Emma kann sie sehen. (wen?)	Emma can see **her**.

Nice to meet	**you**.		*Es freut mich, dich kennen zu lernen.*
How are	**you**?		*Wie geht es dir?*
You can call	**me**	Nikos.	*Du kannst mich Nikos nennen.*
Can you tell	**me**	your name?	*Kannst du mir deinen Namen sagen?*
Rajiv buys a present for	**him**.		*Rajiv kauft ihm ein Geschenk.*
They meet	**him**	at the youth club.	*Sie treffen ihn am Jugendzentrum.*

Subjekt	Objekt	
I	**me**	*mir, mich*
you	**you**	*dir, dich; Ihnen, Sie*
he	**him**	*ihm, ihn*
she	**her**	*ihr, sie*
it	**it**	*ihm, ihn/es*
we	**us**	*uns, uns*
you	**you**	*euch; Ihnen, Sie*
they	**them**	*ihnen, sie*

14 Häufigkeitsadverbien

Wenn man sagen will, wie oft etwas geschieht, benutzt man Häufigkeitsadverbien. Diese Wörter stehen meistens zwischen Subjekt (*wer*) und Verb (siehe LiF 11).

Subjekt *wer*	Adverb *wie oft*	Verb *tut*	Objekt *was*	*(mit wem, wo, wann, usw.)*	
I	**always** **normally** **sometimes** **often** **never**	play	football	with my friends. in the park. in the morning.	*immer* *normalerweise* *manchmal* *oft* *nie*

15 Die Verneinung der einfachen Gegenwart

- Man verneint Sätze in der Gegenwart mit **don't.** Bei *he, she, it* benutzt man **doesn't**. Meistens benutzt man die Kurzformen. Die Langform von *don't* heißt *do not*; die von *doesn't* heißt *does not*.

I	**don't**	play football.
You	**don't**	play tennis.
He	**doesn't**	play cricket.
She	**doesn't**	play hockey.
It	**doesn't**	play with a ball.
We	**don't**	play basketball.
You	**don't**	play cards.
They	**don't**	play games.

Gillian does**n't** play tennis.

David does**n't** like to do his homework.

- Sätze, die Hilfsverben (z. B. *can,* siehe LiF 9) enthalten, werden nicht mit *don't* verneint.

I **can't** find my scarf.
Charlie **isn't** from Hendon. He's from Notting Hill.

16 Fragen in der einfachen Gegenwart: Bestimmungsfragen

- Um zu erfahren, wann, wo, was passiert oder passiert ist, stellt man Bestimmungsfragen.

- Diese Fragen bildet man mit den Fragewörtern:

what	was?
when	wann?
where	wo?
why	warum?
whose	wessen?

- Die Fragewörter stehen immer am Anfang.

What	**does**	he have for breakfast?
When	**do**	you clean your teeth?
Where	**does**	she have breakfast?
Why	**don't**	you listen?
Whose	name has five letters?	

17 Ausnahmen des Plurals

- Die regelmäßigen Pluralformen hast du ja schon in LiF 6 kennen gelernt.
- Hier ein paar Hinweise zu den unregelmäßigen Pluralformen:
  Bei Hauptwörtern (Substantiven), die auf **-y** enden, gilt folgende Regel:

  Steht ein Vokal (*a, e, i, o, u*) vor dem **-y**, wird in der Mehrzahl nur ein **-s** angehängt:
  day ➔ day**s** boy ➔ boy**s**

  Kommt aber ein Konsonant (alle anderen Buchstaben/Laute) vor dem **-y**, dann wird das **-y** zu **-ies**:

  body ➔ bod**ies** pony ➔ pon**ies**

- Aufgepasst: Es gibt einige Wörter, die im Englischen nur die Einzahl oder nur die Mehrzahl bilden.

  Wörter in der Einzahl: food (*Lebensmittel*), homework (*Hausaufgabe/n*), people (*Leute*), bread (*Brot/e*), fish (*Fisch/e*), information (*Information/en*), rubbish (*Müll*), fun (*Spaß*), money (*Geld*)

  Wörter in der Mehrzahl: jeans (*Jeans*), sunglasses (*Sonnenbrille*), clothes (*Kleidung*), news (*Nachricht*)

18 this/that und these/those

- **This** und **that** benutzt man, wenn man zwei Sachen oder Personen unterscheiden will.
  This benutzt man, wenn man über Sachen spricht, die in der Nähe sind. *That* benutzt man für Sachen, die weiter weg sind.
- **These** und **those** sind die Mehrzahlformen von *this* und *that*.

LiF

19 present progressive

- Wenn man sagen möchte, was gerade passiert, benutzt man die Verlaufsform der Gegenwart (*present progressive*).
- Die Verlaufsform bildet man so:

Form von *be* (*am/is/are*) + Verb + *ing*

I	**am**	listen**ing** to music.
You	**are**	stand**ing** on my foot.
He	**is**	do**ing** his homework.
It	**is**	rain**ing.**
We	**are**	watch**ing** TV.

Rajiv **isn't reading** a book.
He **is cleaning** the kitchen.

- Aufgepasst! Besondere Schreibweisen:

Endet ein Verb im Infinitiv auf **-p**, **-t**, **-m**, **-n**, dann wird der Buchstabe verdoppelt:

cut	→ cutting
run	→ running
swim	→ swimming

Endet ein Verb im Infinitv auf **-e**, so fällt das **-e** weg:

make	→ making
dance	→ dancing
take	→ taking

20 Wessen-Fall ('s-Genitiv)

Um zu zeigen, zu wem jemand oder wem etwas gehört, hängt man wie im Deutschen ein **s** (**'s**) an den/die „Besitzer/in". Anders als im Deutschen steht zwischen dem Namen und dem **s** ein Apostroph ('):

David'**s** dog	*Davids Hund*
Caroline'**s** friends	*Carolines Freunde*
Your sister'**s** computer	*Der Computer deiner Schwester*

This is Charlie'**s** sister.

21 Die einfache Vergangenheit (simple past)

- Wenn man etwas erzählen will, das schon vergangen ist – gestern, letzte Woche oder auch letztes Jahr –, benutzt man die einfache Vergangenheit (*simple past*).
  In der einfachen Vergangenheit gibt es nur eine Verbform für alle Personen.
  Die meisten Verben bilden die Vergangenheit (regelmäßige Verben) nach einer Regel.
  Bei manchen Verben trifft diese Regel nicht zu (unregelmäßige Verben).

- Bei regelmäßigen Verben bildet man die Vergangenheit mit -ed, indem man die Endung **-ed** an den Infinitiv anhängt:

I clean my shoes.	*Ich putze meine Schuhe.*
I clean**ed** my shoes.	*Ich habe meine Schuhe geputzt.*

We talk**ed** for hours.	*Wir haben stundenlang geredet.*
Brenda learn**ed** to milk a cow.	*Brenda hat gelernt, eine Kuh zu melken.*
They play**ed** cards with their friends.	*Sie haben Karten mit ihren Freunden gespielt.*

Bei Verben, die im Infinitiv auf **-e** enden, wird nur ein **-d** angehängt.
dance ➔ dance**d**
like ➔ like**d**

- Bei unregelmäßigen Verben wird die Vergangenheit nicht mit -ed gebildet. Man muss ihre Formen wie eine neue Vokabel lernen.

Die Vergangenheit von **be** hat zwei verschieden Formen: **was** und **were**

simple past: be	
I	**was**
you	**were**
he	**was**
she	**was**
it	**was**
we	**were**
you	**were**
they	**were**

Die Vergangenheit von **have** hat nur eine Form: **had**

simple past: have	
I	**had**
you	**had**
he	**had**
she	**had**
it	**had**
we	**had**
you	**had**
they	**had**

Last month

Last month Ivor's hair **was** long.

Now

Now his hair **is** short.

So funktionieren die Wortlisten

Es gibt alphabetische Wortlisten und Wortlisten nach Kapiteln.

Alphabetische Wortlisten

Wenn du nicht mehr weißt, wo ein Wort zum ersten Mal aufgetaucht ist (und es nicht findest), kannst du es in der alphabetischen Wortliste ab **Seite 163** nachschlagen.
Dort findest du auch die Wörter aus allen Arbeitsanweisungen.
Wenn du mal eine Aufgabe machst, bei der du ein „neues" englisches Wort brauchst, kannst du in der deutsch-englischen Wortliste ab **Seite 173** nachgucken.

Wortlisten nach Kapiteln

Vor der Wortliste zu jedem Theme findest du auf den „Say it in English"-Seiten Redewendungen und Wortfelder, die dir in dem Kapitel begegnen.
Hier siehst du, wie du diese Wortlisten (ab **Seite 124**) benutzen kannst:

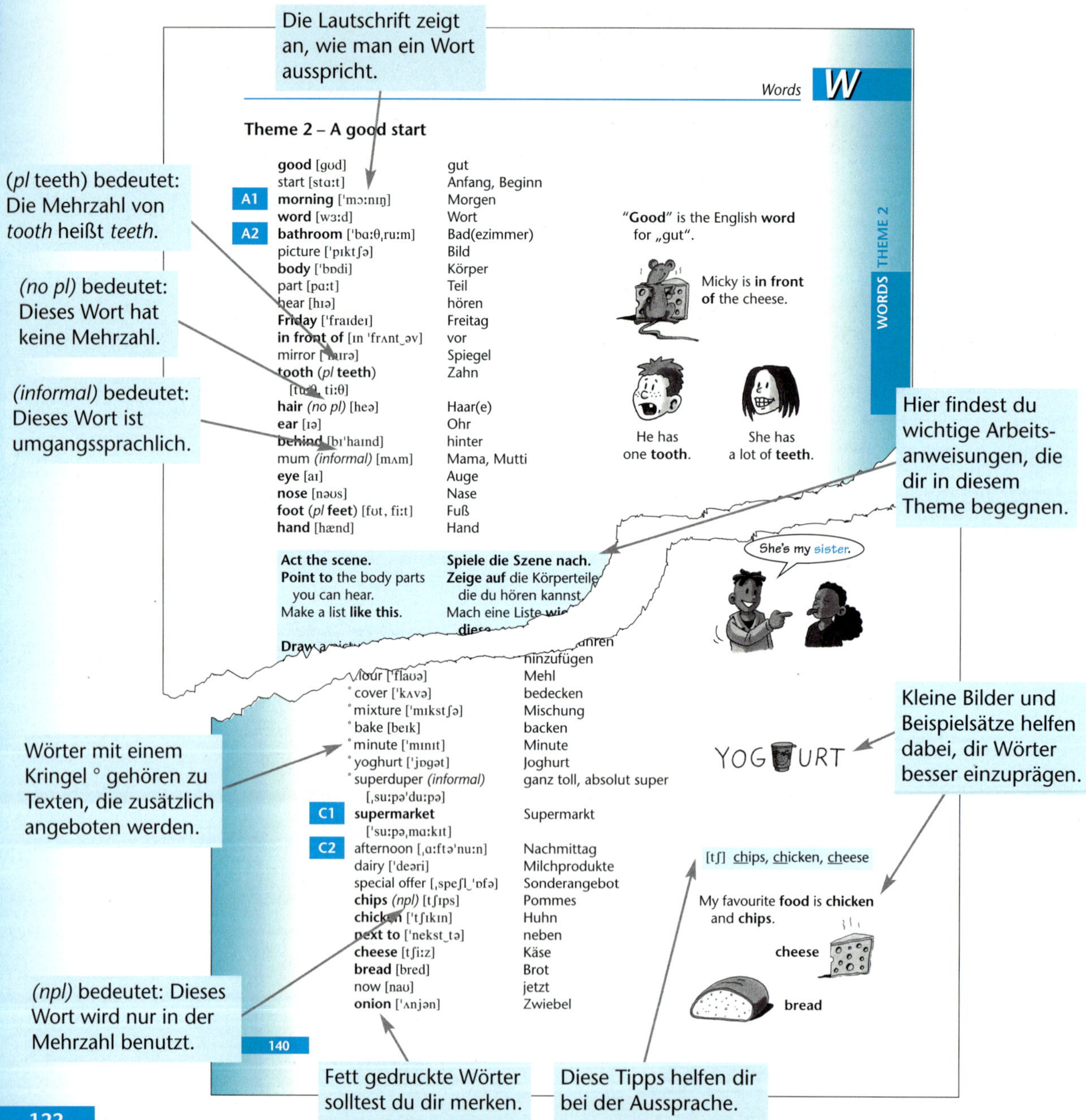

English Sounds

Im Englischen spricht man Wörter oft anders aus, als man sie schreibt. Das ist aber kein Problem. Denn die Aussprache der Wörter ist in jedem Wörterbuch angegeben. So kann man auch neue Wörter richtig aussprechen, ohne sie vorher gehört zu haben.
Dazu nimmt man die so genannte Lautschrift zu Hilfe. Das ist eine Schrift, deren Symbole jeden Laut genau bezeichnen. Die Lautschrift wird in jedem Wörterbuch benutzt.

Hier ist eine Liste mit den Symbolen dieser Lautschrift zusammen mit Beispielwörtern, in denen der entsprechende Laut vorkommt.

Vokale

[ɑː]	**ar**m
[ʌ]	b**u**t
[e]	d**e**sk
[ə]	**a**, **a**n
[ɜː]	g**ir**l, b**ir**d
[æ]	**a**pple
[ɪ]	**i**n, **i**t
[i]	ever**y**
[iː]	**ea**sy, **ea**t
[ɒ]	**o**range, st**o**ry
[ɔː]	**a**ll, c**a**ll
[ʊ]	l**oo**k
[u]	Febr**u**ary
[uː]	f**oo**d

Doppellaute

[aɪ]	**eye**, b**uy**
[aʊ]	**our**
[eə]	th**ere**
[eɪ]	t**a**ke, th**ey**
[ɪə]	h**ere**
[ɔɪ]	b**oy**
[əʊ]	g**o**, **o**ld
[ʊə]	y**ou're**

Konsonanten

[ŋ]	so**ng**, lo**ng**
[r]	**r**ed, **r**ight
[s]	**s**i**s**ter, cla**ss** (scharfes s)
[z]	no**s**e, dog**s** (weiches s)
[dʒ]	oran**ge**
[ʃ]	kit**ch**en
[tʃ]	**ch**ild, **ch**eese
[ð]	**th**ese, mo**th**er (weicher Laut)
[θ]	mou**th**, **th**ink (harter Laut)
[v]	**v**ery, ha**v**e
[w]	**wh**at, **w**ord
[']	Betonungszeichen für die folgende Silbe (Hauptbetonung)
[ˌ]	Betonungszeichen für die folgende Silbe (Nebenbetonung)

The English Alphabet

[eɪ] a	[biː] b	[siː] c	[diː] d	[iː] e	[ef] f
[dʒiː] g	[eɪtʃ] h	[aɪ] i	[dʒeɪ] j	[keɪ] k	[el] l
[em] m	[en] n	[əʊ] o	[piː] p	[kjuː] q	[ɑː] r
[es] s	[tiː] t	[juː] u	[viː] v	['dʌbljuː] w	[eks] x
[waɪ] y	[zed] z				

Welcome

welcome ['welkəm]	willkommen	
I [aɪ]	ich	
I'm (= I am) [aɪm, aɪ‿'æm]	Ich bin; Ich heiße	
hello [hə'ləʊ]	Hallo	
what [wɒt]	was	
your [jɔː]	dein(e)	
name [neɪm]	Name	
What's your name? [ˌwɒts jə 'neɪm]	Wie heißt du?, Wie heißen Sie?	
everyone ['evriwʌn]	jede(r); alle	
Hello everyone! [hə'ləʊ ˌevriwʌn]	Hallo zusammen!	
my [maɪ]	mein(e)	
my name is [maɪ 'neɪm‿ˌɪz]	ich heiße	
a/an [ə, ən]	ein(e)	
Greek [griːk]	Grieche/Griechin; griechisch	

eleven [ɪ'levn]	elf	
have [həv]	haben	
twin [twɪn]	Zwilling, Zwillings-	
brother ['brʌðə]	Bruder	
he [hi]	er	
we [wiː]	wir	
from [frəm]	von, aus	Emma is from London.
new [njuː]	neu	
in [ɪn]	in	
live [lɪv]	leben, wohnen	
small [smɔːl]	klein	
house [haʊs]	Haus	
with [wɪð]	mit	
our [aʊə]	unser(e)	
mum *(informal)* [mʌm]	Mama, Mutti	
dad *(informal)* [dæd]	Papa, Vati	

like [laɪk]	mögen	
inline skating *(no pl)* [ˌɪnlaɪn 'skeɪtɪŋ]	Inline-Skaten	
dancing ['dɑːnsɪŋ]	Tanzen	
and [ənd]	und	
animal ['ænɪml]	Tier	
cat [kæt]	Katze	Caroline has a cat. Her name is Socks.
her [hɜː]	ihr(e, n)	
sock [sɒk]	Socke	
she [ʃɪ]	sie	
basket ['bɑːskɪt]	Korb	
room [ruːm]	Zimmer, Raum	

too [tuː]	auch	Caroline has a cat. Gillian has a cat, too.
favourite ['feɪv(ə)rət]	Lieblings-	
food *(no pl)* [fuːd]	Essen	
drink [drɪŋk]	Getränk	My favourite food is chips.
coke [kəʊk]	Cola	
say [seɪ]	sagen	
milk [mɪlk]	Milch	
good [gʊd]	gut	
for [fɔː]	für	
ugh *(informal)* [ʌg]	i!, igitt!	milk
you [jʊ]	dich	
music ['mjuːzɪk]	Musik	
or [ɔː]	oder	
school [skuːl]	Schule	
go [gəʊ]	gehen	
street [striːt]	Straße	
really ['rɪəli]	wirklich	
nice [naɪs]	schön; nett	
tea [tiː]	Tee	tea
sugar ['ʃʊgə]	Zucker	
plan [plæn]	Plan	
tomorrow [tə'mɒrəʊ]	morgen	
meet [miːt]	(sich) treffen	
friend [frend]	Freund/in	Emma and Caroline are friends.
the [ðə]	der/die/das	

[uː] t<u>oo</u>, f<u>oo</u>d, sch<u>oo</u>l
[iː] str<u>ee</u>t, t<u>ea</u>, m<u>ee</u>t

Theme 1 • Friends

Say it in English

So kann man …

jemanden begrüßen	Hi! Hello.
sich oder jemand anderes vorstellen	I'm Rajiv./My name is …/This is Caroline.
jemanden nach dem Namen fragen	What's your name?
fragen/sagen, wo jemand herkommt	Where are you from? – I'm from Manchester./ She's/He's from …
einen Vorschlag machen	What about …?/Let's …
einem Vorschlag zustimmen	Yes, good idea.
einen Vorschlag ablehnen	No, thanks.
sich entschuldigen	Sorry!/I'm sorry./I'm very sorry!
sagen, was man mag	I like …
auf Gegenstände/Personen verweisen	There is/There are …
Gegenstände oder Personen beschreiben	Her bike is …/Their clothes are …
nach dem Alter fragen – und darauf antworten	How old are you? – I'm eleven.
über die Uhrzeit sprechen	What time is it, please? – It's three o'clock./It's 9:20.

Word field

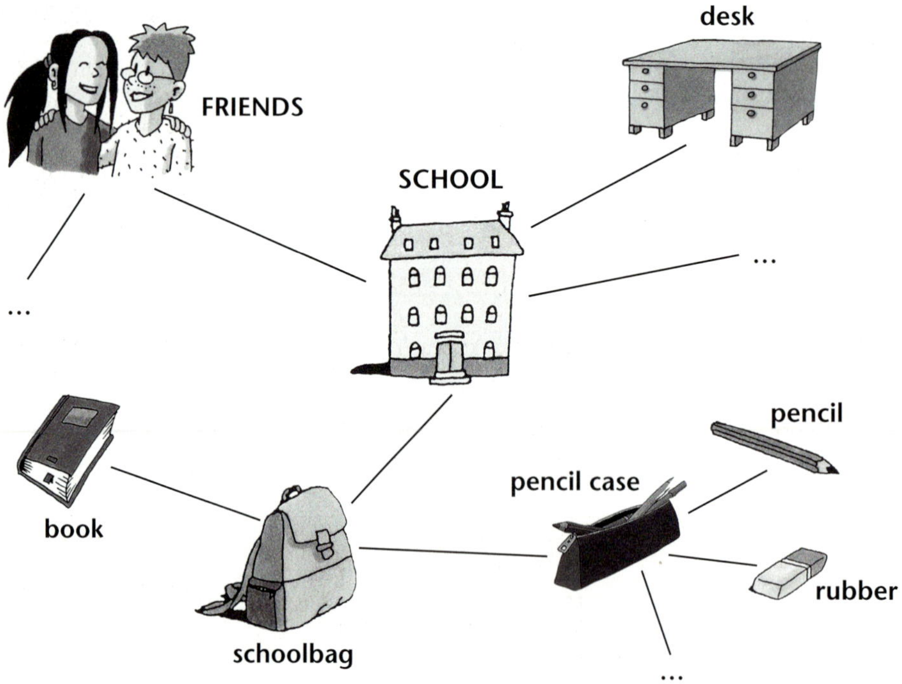

theme (1) [θiːm (wʌn)]	Kapitel (1)	Emma and Caroline are **friends**.
friend [frend]	Freund/in	
who [huː]	wer, wem, wen	**Who** is Emma? – Emma is Caroline's **friend**.
be [biː]	sein	
the [ðə]	der/die/das	
girl [gɜːl]	Mädchen	
with [wɪð]	mit	
everyone ['evriˌwʌn]	jede(r); alle	
this [ðɪs]	diese(r, s); das	
she [ʃɪ]	sie	Gillian is a **girl**. **She** is from Notting Hill.
new [njuː]	neu	
here [hɪə]	hier	
from [frəm]	von, aus	

Work with a partner.	**Arbeite mit einem/einer Partner/in zusammen.**
Find ten things.	**Finde** zehn Dinge.
What can you see/hear/find out/...?	**Was kannst du** sehen/hören/herausfinden/...?
Listen to the CD.	**Höre** die CD **an**.
Talk about the friends/your picture/...	**Rede über** die Freunde/dein Bild/...
Write about what you like/your card/...	**Schreibe** über das, was du magst/deine Karte/...
Ask your partner/...	**Frage** deine/n Partner/in/...
Read the text/...	**Lies** den Text/...
Look at the word list/**pages** 22/23/...	**Sieh in** die Wortliste/**auf** die **Seiten** 22/23/...
Say what you like.	**Sag**, was du magst.
Make a class survey/...	**Mache** eine Umfrage in der Klasse/...

friends

hello [hə'ləʊ]	hallo	
I [aɪ]	ich	
I'm (= **I am**) [aɪm, aɪ‿'æm]	Ich bin; Ich heiße	
and [ənd]	und	
What about ...? *(informal)* [ˌwɒt‿ə'baʊt]	Was ist mit ...?, Wie wäre es mit ...?	**What about** a game of **football**? – Oh, **yes**!
a/an [ə,ən]	ein(e)	
game [geɪm]	Spiel	
football *(no pl)* ['fʊtbɔːl]	Fußball	
think [θɪŋk]	denken, glauben, meinen	
yes [jes]	ja	
that [ðæt]	der/die/das (da drüben)	
good [gʊd]	gut	
idea [aɪ'dɪə]	Idee	
we [wiː]	wir	

	play [pleɪ]	spielen
	over there [ˌəʊvə 'ðeə]	dort drüben
	go [gəʊ]	gehen
	Let's go. [lets 'gəʊ]	Los!
A1	sing along [ˌsɪŋ‿ə'lɒŋ]	mitsingen
	look at ['lʊk‿æt]	betrachten, sehen
	picture ['pɪktʃə]	Bild
	thing [θɪŋ]	Ding, Gegenstand
	see [siː]	sehen
A2	**in** [ɪn]	in
	now [naʊ]	jetzt
A3	**he** [hi]	er
	where [weə]	wo
	they [ðeɪ]	sie
	all [ɔːl]	alle(s)
A4	your [jɔː]	dein(e)
	name [neɪm]	Name
	What's your name? [ˌwɒts jə 'neɪm]	Wie heißt du?, Wie heißen Sie?
	my [maɪ]	meine(e)
	my name is [maɪ 'neɪm‿ˌɪz]	ich heiße
	Where are you from? [ˌweər‿ɑː jə 'frɒm]	Wo kommst du her?
A5	word [wɜːd]	Wort
	for [fɔː]	für
	again [ə'gen]	wieder; noch einmal
	ice cream [ˌaɪs 'kriːm]	Eiskrem, Eis
	no [nəʊ]	nein
	thanks [θæŋks]	danke
	not [nɒt]	nicht
	cake [keɪk]	Kuchen
	orange juice ['ɒrɪndʒ ˌdʒuːs]	Orangensaft
	apple ['æpl]	Apfel
A6	meet [miːt]	(sich) treffen
	people *(pl)* ['piːpl]	Leute
	Germany ['dʒɜːməni]	Deutschland
A7	**classroom** ['klɑːsˌruːm]	Klassenzimmer
	of [əv]	von
	favourite ['feɪv(ə)rət]	Lieblings-
	this is ['ðɪs‿ɪz]	das ist/sind
	prince [prɪns]	Prinz
	England ['ɪŋglənd]	England
	classmate ['klɑːsˌmeɪt]	Klassenkamerad/in
A8	**to** [tə]	in, nach, zu, an
	how [haʊ]	wie
	How are you? [haʊ‿'ɑː ˌjʊ]	Wie geht es dir/Ihnen/euch?
	great [greɪt]	großartig, wunderbar
	I've made new friends already. [aɪv ˌmeɪd njuː ˌfrendz‿ɔːl'redi]	Ich habe schon neue Freunde gefunden.
	make friends [meɪk 'frendz]	sich anfreunden

They are **playing** a game.

I can **see** David. **He is over there.**

Where are you from? – I'm from London.

What about an **ice cream**? – **No, thanks,** not now.

This is our **classroom.**

My **favourite** drink is coke.

classmates = people in my **class.**

	already [ɔːl'redi]	schon
	boy [bɔɪ]	Junge
	like [laɪk]	mögen
	their [ðeə]	ihr(e)
	too [tuː]	auch
	our [aʊə]	unser(e)
	together [tə'geðə]	zusammen, gemeinsam
	music ['mjuːzɪk]	Musik
	have [həv]	haben
	a lot (of) [ə 'lɒt (əv)]	viel(e)
	must [mʌst]	müssen
	tell [tel]	erzählen; *hier:* sagen
	so [səʊ]	so
	nice [naɪs]	schön, nett
	back [bæk]	zurück
	book [bʊk]	Buch
	because [bɪ'kɒz]	weil
	pet [pet]	Haustier
	dog [dɒg]	Hund
	its [ɪts]	sein(e), ihr(e)
	funny ['fʌni]	lustig, witzig, komisch
	cat [kæt]	Katze
	her [hɜː]	ihr(e, n)

Colours

black [blæk]	schwarz
blue [bluː]	blau
brown [braʊn]	braun
golden ['gəʊldn]	golden
green [griːn]	grün
grey [greɪ]	grau
orange ['ɒrɪndʒ]	orange(farben)
purple ['pɜːpl]	violett
red [red]	rot
white [waɪt]	weiß
yellow ['jeləʊ]	gelb

	president ['prezɪdənt]	Präsident/in
	goldfish (*pl* **goldfish**) ['gəʊld,fɪʃ]	Goldfisch
	exciting [ɪk'saɪtɪŋ]	aufregend; spannend
	well [wel]	nun (ja), tja
	finish ['fɪnɪʃ]	beenden, aufhören
	CU (= See you.) ['siː jə]	Bis bald.
A9	sometimes ['sʌmtaɪmz]	manchmal
	often ['ɒfn]	oft, häufig
A10	**rabbit** ['ræbɪt]	Kaninchen
B1	**market** ['mɑːkɪt]	Markt
	buy [baɪ]	kaufen
B2	**at** [æt]	auf

I **like** ice cream and my brother **likes** ice cream, **too**.

Gillian has **a lot of** CDs.

This is a **great book**!

We **have** a **nice dog**. **Its** name is Spot.

cat

Her name is Fuzzy.

goldfish

goldfish

rabbit

WORDS THEME 1

	street [striːt]	Straße
	stall [stɔːl]	(Verkaufs)stand
	there is/are [ðeər‿'ɪz/'ɑː]	es gibt, da sind
	sunglasses *(npl)* ['sʌnˌglɑːsɪz]	Sonnenbrille
	other ['ʌðə]	andere(r, s)
	it [ɪt]	es
	his [hɪs]	sein(e, r)
	Mr ['mɪstə]	Herr *(Anrede)*
	shop [ʃɒp]	Geschäft, Laden

There are T-shirts **at** the street market.

she he **it**

Numbers

1 **one** [wʌn]	17 seventeen [ˌsevn'tiːn]
2 **two** [tuː]	18 eighteen [ˌeɪ'tiːn]
3 **three** [θriː]	19 nineteen [ˌnaɪn'tiːn]
4 **four** [fɔː]	20 twenty ['twenti]
5 **five** [faɪv]	21 twenty-one [ˌtwenti'wʌn]
6 **six** [sɪks]	...
7 **seven** ['sevn]	30 thirty ['θɜːti]
8 **eight** [eɪt]	40 forty ['fɔːti]
9 **nine** [naɪn]	50 fifty ['fɪfti]
10 **ten** [ten]	60 sixty ['sɪksti]
11 **eleven** [ɪ'levn]	70 seventy ['sevnti]
12 **twelve** [twelv]	80 eighty ['eɪti]
13 thirteen [ˌθɜː'tiːn]	90 ninety ['naɪnti]
14 fourteen [ˌfɔː'tiːn]	100 one hundred [ˌwʌn 'hʌndrəd]
15 fifteen [ˌfɪf'tiːn]	
16 sixteen [ˌsɪks'tiːn]	

Her name is Mandy. **His** name is Nino.

bike

B4	more [mɔː]	mehr
	school [skuːl]	Schule
	on [ɒn]	auf
	or [ɔː]	oder
B5	last [lɑːst]	letzte(r, s)
	day [deɪ]	Tag
	holidays *(npl)* ['hɒlɪdeɪz]	Ferien, Urlaub
	boat [bəʊt]	Boot
	bike [baɪk]	(Fahr)rad
	hat [hæt]	Hut
	clothes *(npl)* [kləʊðz]	Kleider, Kleidung
B6	**class** [klɑːs]	(Schul)klasse
	wrong [rɒŋ]	falsch
	right [raɪt]	richtig
B7	count [kaʊnt]	zählen
	up [ʌp]	nach oben
	old [əʊld]	alt
	work [wɜːk]	*hier:* funktionieren
	any more [ˌeni 'mɔː]	nicht mehr
	watch out for [ˌwɒtʃ‿'aʊt fə]	Ausschau halten nach
	number ['nʌmbə]	Zahl; Ziffer; Nummer

clothes

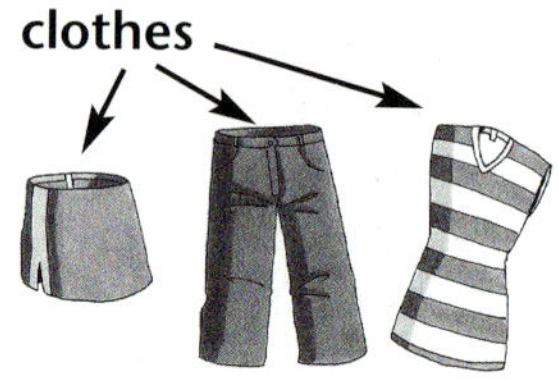

Jeans and T-shirts are **clothes**.

There are twelve boys and eight girls in my **class**.

8 + 7 = 15 ✓ 6 + 11 = 14 ✗

right **wrong**

[ɑː] last, class, start
[ʌ] other, up, number

	then [ðen]	dann	
	start [stɑːt]	anfangen	
	glasses *(npl)* ['glɑːsɪz]	Brille	
	child *(pl* children) [tʃaɪld, 'tʃɪldrən]	Kind	
	yummy *(informal)* ['jʌmi]	lecker	
	melon ['melən]	Melone	
	shelf *(pl* shelves) [ʃelf, ʃelvz]	Regal	
B9	year [jɪə]	Jahr	
	lucky number [ˌlʌki 'nʌmbə]	Glückszahl	
C1	time [taɪm]	(Uhr)zeit	
	What time is it? [ˌwɒt‿taɪm‿'ɪz‿ɪt]	Wie viel Uhr ist es?	**What time is it?** – It's ten.
	German ['dʒɜːmən]	deutsch	
	schoolbag ['skuːlbæg]	Schultasche	
	sorry ['sɒri]	Verzeihung, Entschuldigung	
	Do you have …? [ˌduː juː 'hæv]	Hast du/Haben Sie …?	
	please [pliːz]	bitte	
	late [leɪt]	(zu) spät	
	ruler ['ruːlə]	Lineal	
	Here you are. [ˌhɪə juː‿'ɑː]	Hier, bitte!, Bitte schön!	Can you give me a **ruler**, please? – Yes, **here you are**.
	pen [pen]	Stift	
	but [bət]	aber	
	pencil ['pensl]	Bleistift	
C2	**board** [bɔːd]	Tafel	Can you write the answer on the **board**?
	chair [tʃeə]	Stuhl	
	desk [desk]	Schreibtisch	
	door [dɔː]	Tür	
	rubber ['rʌbə]	Radiergummi	
	exercise book ['eksəsaɪz ˌbʊk]	Heft	Where's your **exercise book**? – It's in my schoolbag.
	felt-tip [ˌfelt'tɪp]	Filzstift	
	folder ['fəʊldə]	Mappe, Schnellhefter	
	pencil case ['pensl ˌkeɪs]	Federmäppchen	
	window ['wɪndəʊ]	Fenster	
	English ['ɪŋglɪʃ]	englisch	
C3	dream [driːm]	Traum	
C6	**(three) o'clock** [(θriː) ə'klɒk]	(drei) Uhr	
C8	me [miː]	mir, mich	
	stick [stɪk]	kleben	
	photo ['fəʊtəʊ]	Foto	
	phone [fəʊn]	Telefon	
	colour ['kʌlə]	Farbe	
	record [rɪ'kɔːd]	aufnehmen	

ruler

rubber

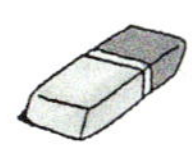

pencil case

door

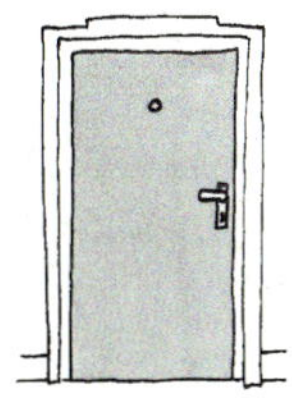

WORDS THEME 1

O	°British ['brɪtɪʃ]	britisch
	°yard [jɑːd]	(Hinter)hof
	°skipping *(no pl)* ['skɪpɪŋ]	Seilspringen
	°rhyme *(no pl)* [raɪm]	Reim
	°coffee ['kɒfi]	Kaffee
	°tea [tiː]	Tee
	°person ['pɜːsn]	Person, Mensch
	°jump [dʒʌmp]	springen
	°crocodile ['krɒkəˌdaɪl]	Krokodil
	°cross [krɒs]	durchqueren; überqueren
	°river ['rɪvə]	Fluss
	°reply [rɪ'plaɪ]	antworten
	°something ['sʌmθɪŋ]	etwas
	°like [laɪk]	wie
	°if [ɪf]	falls
	°wear [weə]	tragen
	°move on [muːv‿'ɒn]	sich wieder auf den Weg machen; weitergehen
	°step [step]	Schritt
	°when [wen]	wenn
	°reach [riːtʃ]	erreichen
	°side [saɪd]	Seite
	°next [nekst]	nächste(r, s)
	°September [sep'tembə]	September
	°October [ɒk'təʊbə]	Oktober
	°hit [hɪt]	(zu)schlagen
	°conker ['kɒŋkə]	Rosskastanie
	°hard [hɑːd]	hart; *hier:* kräftig
	°in turns [ɪn 'tɜːnz]	abwechselnd
	°best [best]	beste(r, s)
	°win [wɪn]	gewinnen
	°find out about [faɪnd‿'aʊt‿əˌbaʊt]	sich informieren über
	°rule [ruːl]	Regel
	°first [fɜːst]	erste(r, s)
	°clap [klæp]	klatschen
	°hand [hænd]	Hand
	°sailor ['seɪlə]	Matrose, Seemann
	°sea *(no pl)* [siː]	Meer
	°go to sea [ˌgəʊ tə 'siː]	zur See gehen
	°bottom ['bɒtəm]	Grund
	°deep [diːp]	tief
	°Chinese [ˌtʃaɪ'niːz]	Chinese/Chinesin; chinesisch
	°restaurant ['rest(ə)rɒnt]	Restaurant
	°loaf of bread [ˌləʊf‿əv 'bred]	Brotlaib
	°poodle ['puːdl]	Pudel
	°whisker ['wɪskə]	Schnurrhaar
	°freeze [friːz]	gefrieren; einfrieren

Zehn Minuten
Übe die Vokabeln immer nur fünf bis zehn Minuten, aber dafür regelmäßig! Das ist viel wirkungsvoller als eine ganze Stunde, die aber nur zweimal im Monat. Probiere dabei die Vokabeltipps auf den nächsten Seiten aus.

crocodile

Wortkarten
Besorge dir 20 bis 30 kleine Karteikarten oder schneide dir welche zurecht. Schreibe einzelne Vokabeln auf die Kärtchen – auf der einen Seite auf Deutsch, auf der anderen Seite auf Englisch. Das ist deine Lernkartei! Du kannst die Wörter mal Englisch-Deutsch und mal Deutsch-Englisch üben. Vergiss nicht, die Karten immer neu zu mischen! Und mit einem Gummiband darum werden sie sogar zur tragbaren Lernkartei.

[æ] cl<u>a</u>p, h<u>a</u>nd

Theme 2 • A good start

Say it in English

So kann man …

sagen, dass etwas stimmt/nicht stimmt	Yes, that's right./No, that's wrong./ That's not right.
fragen, wo sich etwas befindet	Where's the …?
fragen, was etwas auf Deutsch/ Englisch heißt	What's … in German/English?/ What's the English/German word for …?
jemandem seine Hilfe anbieten	Can I help you?/What can I do for you?
höflich auf sich aufmerksam machen	Excuse me.
sich bedanken	Thank you./Thanks./Thank you very much.
fragen/sagen, wie viel etwas kostet	How much is the pullover? – It's £8. How much are these apples? – They're £1 a kilo.
jemanden etwas geben	Here you are.
sich verabschieden	Bye./See you.

Word field

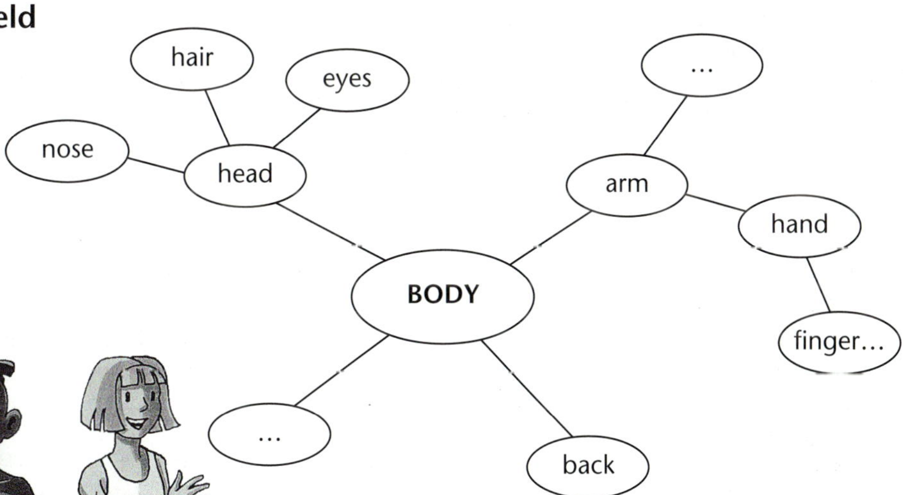

tall
strong
short
good-looking
beautiful
blond
…

	good [gʊd]	gut
	start [stɑːt]	Anfang, Beginn
A1	**morning** ['mɔːnɪŋ]	Morgen
	word [wɜːd]	Wort
A2	**bathroom** ['bɑːθˌruːm]	Bad(ezimmer)
	picture ['pɪktʃə]	Bild
	body ['bɒdi]	Körper
	part [pɑːt]	Teil
	hear [hɪə]	hören
	Friday ['fraɪdeɪ]	Freitag
	in front of [ɪn 'frʌnt‿əv]	vor
	mirror ['mɪrə]	Spiegel
	tooth (*pl* **teeth**) [tuːθ, tiːθ]	Zahn
	hair *(no pl)* [heə]	Haar(e)
	ear [ɪə]	Ohr
	behind [bɪ'haɪnd]	hinter
	mum *(informal)* [mʌm]	Mama, Mutti
	eye [aɪ]	Auge
	nose [nəʊs]	Nase
	foot (*pl* **feet**) [fʊt, fiːt]	Fuß
	hand [hænd]	Hand

"**Good**" is the English **word** for „gut".

Micky is **in front of** the cheese.

He has one **tooth**.

She has a lot of **teeth**.

Act the scene.	**Spiele die Szene nach.**
Point to the body parts you can hear.	**Zeige auf** die Körperteile, die du hören kannst.
Make a list **like this**.	Mach eine Liste **wie diese**.
Draw a picture/pictures.	**Zeichne** ein Bild/Bilder.
Can you find the answers/…?	**Kannst du** die Antworten finden/…?
Present your poem **to** the class.	**Präsentiere** dein Gedicht **vor** der Klasse.
Describe other people to a partner.	**Beschreibe** deinem/deiner Partner/in andere Leute.
Who are the people?	**Wer** sind die Leute?
Play the (shopping) **game**.	**Spiele** das (Einkaufs)**spiel**.

Micky is **behind** the cheese.

English **breakfast**

Come on! [kʌm‿'ɒn]	Komm jetzt!, Mach schon!
breakfast ['brekfəst]	Frühstück
table ['teɪbl]	Tisch
water *(no pl)* ['wɔːtə]	Wasser
sea *(no pl)* [siː]	Meer
but [bət]	aber
hurry up [ˌhʌri‿'ʌp]	sich beeilen
go [gəʊ]	gehen
work *(no pl)* [wɜːk]	Arbeit
forget [fə'get]	vergessen

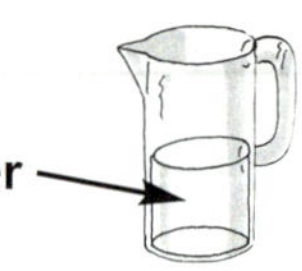

I like apples, **but** my friend likes oranges.

	shopping *(no pl)* [ˈʃɒpɪŋ]	Einkaufen
	after [ˈɑːftə]	nach
	shopping list [ˈʃɒpɪŋ ˌlɪst]	Einkaufsliste
	mother [ˈmʌðə]	Mutter
	must [mʌst]	müssen
	that [ðæt]	der/die/das (da drüben)
A3	**them** [ðem]	sie, ihnen
	for [fɔː]	für
A4	**head** [hed]	Kopf
	neck [nek]	Nacken
	face [feɪs]	Gesicht
	tummy [ˈtʌmi]	Bauch
	toe [təʊ]	Zeh(e)
	thumb [θʌm]	Daumen
	mouth [maʊθ]	Mund
	arm [ɑːm]	Arm
	shoulder [ˈʃəʊldə]	Schulter
	finger [ˈfɪŋgə]	Finger
	elbow [ˈelbəʊ]	Ellbogen
	back [bæk]	Rücken
	bottom [ˈbɒtəm]	Hinterteil
	leg [leg]	Bein
	knee [niː]	Knie
	or [ɔː]	oder
A5	wash [wɒʃ]	waschen
	me [miː]	ich
	up [ʌp]	nach oben
	straight [streɪt]	gerade(aus)
	on top of [ɒn ˈtɒp‿əv]	auf
	half [hɑːf]	halb
	open [ˈəʊpən]	offen, geöffnet
	take [teɪk]	(mit)nehmen
	toothbrush [ˈtuːθˌbrʌʃ]	Zahnbürste
	toothpaste [ˈtuːθˌpeɪst]	Zahnpasta
	hairbrush [ˈheəˌbrʌʃ]	Haarbürste
	comb [kəʊm]	Kamm
	soap [səʊp]	Seife
	toilet bag [ˈtɔɪlət ˌbæg]	Kulturbeutel, Toilettentasche
	neat [niːt]	ordentlich, sauber
	ev'ry (= every) [ˈevri]	jede(r, s)
	rinse [rɪns]	spülen
	all [ɔːl]	ganz, völlig
	dirt *(no pl)* [dɜːt]	Schmutz
	away [əˈweɪ]	weg
	time [taɪm]	(Uhr)zeit
	bed [bed]	Bett
	so [səʊ]	so
	dirty [ˈdɜːti]	dreckig, schmutzig

Gegensätze
Neue Vokabeln musst du nicht immer in Listen schreiben. Du kannst sie auch anders sortieren, zum Beispiel indem du Gegensätze zusammen stellst. Wie viele Wörter kennst du schon, die sich in dieser Weise zusammen stellen lassen?

Beispiele:
girl – boy
black – white
right – wrong

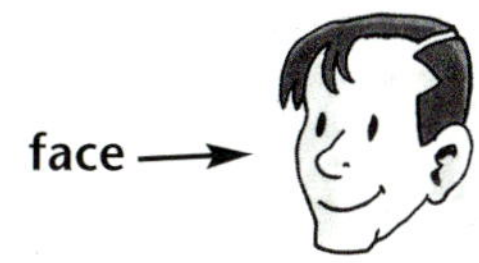

Spiders have eight **legs**.

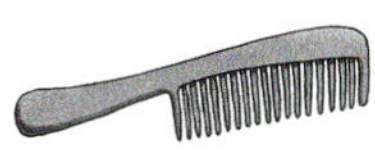

What is it?

[heə]
[aɪ] [aɪ]
[nəʊs]
[maʊθ]

	where [weə]	wo
	furry ['fɜːri]	pelzig
	should [ʃʊd]	sollen
	do [duː]	machen, tun
	choose [tʃuːz]	auswählen
A6	hate [heɪt]	hassen
	still [stɪl]	(immer) noch
	big [bɪg]	groß
	long [lɒŋ]	lang
	ugly ['ʌgli]	hässlich
	good-looking [ˌgʊd'lʊkɪŋ]	gut aussehend
	guy [gaɪ]	Kerl, Typ
	tall [tɔːl]	groß
	strong [strɒŋ]	stark
	slim [slɪm]	schlank, schmal, dünn
	short [ʃɔːt]	kurz
	dark [dɑːk]	dunkel
	small [smɔːl]	klein
	That's me [ðæts 'miː]	Das bin ich
	Mr ['mɪstə]	Herr *(Anrede)*
	perfect ['pɜːfɪkt]	vollkommen, perfekt
	dictionary ['dɪkʃənri]	Wörterbuch
A7	people *(pl)* ['piːpl]	Leute
	old [əʊld]	alt
	man (*pl* **men**) [mæn, men]	Mann
	woman (*pl* **women**) ['wʊmən, 'wɪmɪn]	Frau
	straight [streɪt]	gerade; *hier:* glatt
A8	poem ['pəʊɪm]	Gedicht
	brother ['brʌðə]	Bruder
	someone ['sʌmwʌn]	jemand
B1	What's for breakfast? [ˌwɒts fə 'brekfəst]	Was gibt's zum Frühstück?
	have [hæv]	*hier:* essen; trinken
	food *(no pl)* [fuːd]	Essen, Nahrung
	drink [drɪŋk]	Getränk
B2	**Saturday** ['sætədeɪ]	Samstag, Sonnabend
	dining-room ['daɪnɪŋ ˌruːm]	Esszimmer
	coffee ['kɒfi]	Kaffee
	here [hɪə]	hier
	ready ['redi]	fertig
	late [leɪt]	(zu) spät
	milk [mɪlk]	Milch
	on [ɒn]	auf
	sugar ['ʃʊgə]	Zucker
	yup *(informal)* [jʌp]	ja
	bacon ['beɪkən]	(Schinken)speck

He is **strong**.

tall

short

He is **old**.

man

woman

Charlie **has** cornflakes for breakfast.

My favourite **drink** is coke.

Coffee and **milk** are **drinks**.

milk

Micky is **on** the cheese.

	egg [eg]	Ei
	baked beans [ˌbeɪkt ˈbiːnz]	Baked Beans *(Bohnen in Tomatensauce)*
	sausage [ˈsɒsɪdʒ]	Wurst, Würstchen
	marmalade *(no pl)* [ˈmɑːməˌleɪd]	*Marmelade aus Zitrusfrüchten*
	cupboard [ˈkʌbəd]	Schrank
	cereal *(no pl)* [ˈsɪəriəl]	Frühstückszerealien *(Cornflakes, Müsli …)*
	mushroom [ˈmʌʃruːm]	Pilz
	jam [dʒæm]	Marmelade
B3	**Monday** [ˈmʌndeɪ]	Montag
B4	**eat** [iːt]	essen
	before [bɪˈfɔː]	vor
	weekend [ˌwiːkˈend]	Wochenende
B5	**tea** [tiː]	Tee
	all [ɔːl]	alle(s)
	sister [ˈsɪstə]	Schwester
	orange [ˈɒrɪndʒ]	Orange
	kitchen [ˈkɪtʃən]	Küche
B6	°butter [ˈbʌtə]	Butter
	°preheat (to) [priːˈhiːt (tə)]	vorheizen (auf)
	°oven [ˈʌvn]	(Back)ofen, Backrohr
	°put [pʊt]	setzen, stellen, legen
	°some [sʌm]	einige; etwas
	°cake pan [ˈkeɪk ˌpæn]	Kuchenform
	°cut [kʌt]	schneiden
	°cinnamon [ˈsɪnəmən]	Zimt
	°beat [biːt]	*hier:* verrühren
	°add [æd]	hinzufügen
	°flour [ˈflaʊə]	Mehl
	°cover [ˈkʌvə]	bedecken
	°mixture [ˈmɪkstʃə]	Mischung
	°bake [beɪk]	backen
	°minute [ˈmɪnɪt]	Minute
	°yoghurt [ˈjɒgət]	Joghurt
	°superduper *(informal)* [ˌsuːpəˈduːpə]	ganz toll, absolut super
C1	**supermarket** [ˈsuːpəˌmɑːkɪt]	Supermarkt
C2	afternoon [ˌɑːftəˈnuːn]	Nachmittag
	dairy [ˈdeəri]	Milchprodukte
	special offer [ˌspeʃl‿ˈɒfə]	Sonderangebot
	chips *(npl)* [tʃɪps]	Pommes
	chicken [ˈtʃɪkɪn]	Huhn
	next to [ˈnekst‿tə]	neben
	cheese [tʃiːz]	Käse
	bread [bred]	Brot
	now [naʊ]	jetzt
	onion [ˈʌnjən]	Zwiebel

egg

sausage

jam

tea

[tʃ] chips, chicken, cheese

My favourite **food** is **chicken** and **chips**.

cheese

bread

	vegetable ['vedʒtəbl]	Gemüse	
	shop assistant ['ʃɒp‿əˌsɪstnt]	Verkäufer/in	
	right [raɪt]	gut, ok	
	door [dɔː]	Tür	
	so [səʊ]	also	
	orange juice *(no pl)* ['ɒrɪndʒ ˌdʒuːs]	Orangensaft	
	bottle ['bɒtl]	Flasche	
	lady ['leɪdi]	Frau, Dame	Can you give me a pen? **Thank you.**
	thank you ['θæŋk ˌjə]	danke	
	frozen ['frəʊzn]	(tief)gefroren	
	freezer ['friːzə]	Gefrierschrank	
	magazine [ˌmægə'ziːn]	Zeitschrift, Magazin	
	sure [ʃɔː]	sicher	
	not mind [nɒt 'maɪnd]	nichts dagegen haben	
C4	**pound** [paʊnd]	Pfund	
	penny (*pl* **pence**) [peni, pens]	Penny	
	get [get]	erhalten, bekommen	At the supermarket you can **get** bread.
	free [friː]	frei, gratis	
C5	how much [ˌhaʊ 'mʌtʃ]	wie viel	
	add [æd]	hinzufügen	
	thing [θɪŋ]	Ding, Gegenstand	
	price [praɪs]	Preis	
	How much is/are …? [ˌhaʊ mʌtʃ‿'ɪz/'ɑː]	Was kostet/kosten …?	**How much is** this pullover, **please**? – **It's** £10.
	it's [ɪts]	*hier:* er/sie/es kostet	**How much are** the apples? – **They are** £2.
	they are [ðeɪ‿'ɑː]	*hier:* sie kosten	
C6	at the baker's [ˌæt ðə 'beɪkəz]	in der Bäckerei, beim Bäcker	
	help [help]	helfen	
	roll [rəʊl]	Brötchen	
	Anything else? [ˌeniθɪŋ‿'els]	Darf es noch etwas sein?	
	that's [ðæts]	*hier:* das kostet	Here's your roll. **That's** 20p.
	bye *(informal)* [baɪ]	tschüs	
O1	°crazy ['kreɪzi]	verrückt	
	°project ['prɒdʒekt]	Projekt	
	°potato (*pl* -es) [pə'teɪtəʊ, pə'teɪtəʊz]	Kartoffel	
	°banana [bə'nɑːnə]	Banane	
	°collect [kə'lekt]	sammeln	
	°exhibition [ˌeksɪ'bɪʃn]	Ausstellung	
O2	°traffic ['træfɪk]	Verkehr	
	°traffic jam ['træfɪk ˌdʒæm]	Stau	
	°hand of the clock [hænd‿əv ðə klɒk]	Uhrzeiger	
	°fish finger [ˌfɪʃ 'fɪŋgə]	Fischstäbchen	

Vokabeln umschreiben
Wenn du dir manche Wörter einfach nicht merken kannst, versuche Folgendes: Überlege dir, was das Wort bedeutet und schreibe dir einen kleinen englischen Satz dazu auf, zum Beispiel: *classmates = people in my class.*

Theme 3 • Free time

Say it in English

So kann man …

jemanden fragen, ob er/sie etwas kann	Can you speak English?/Can Caroline come?
jemandem sagen, dass man etwas tun kann	I can speak English./I can give you a scarf.
sagen, was jemand nicht tun kann	Mary can't come.
ausdrücken, dass man etwas mit Spannung erwartet	I can't wait./I'm so excited.
sagen, dass einem etwas Leid tut	I'm sorry.
jemanden beschreiben	She has blue eyes.
jemandem etwas erlauben	You can give the hedgehog some water.
jemandem etwas verbieten	No, you can't give milk to a hedgehog.
jemanden fragen, ob er/sie etwas besitzt	Do you have a pet?
sagen, dass man etwas besitzt	I have a hamster.

Word field

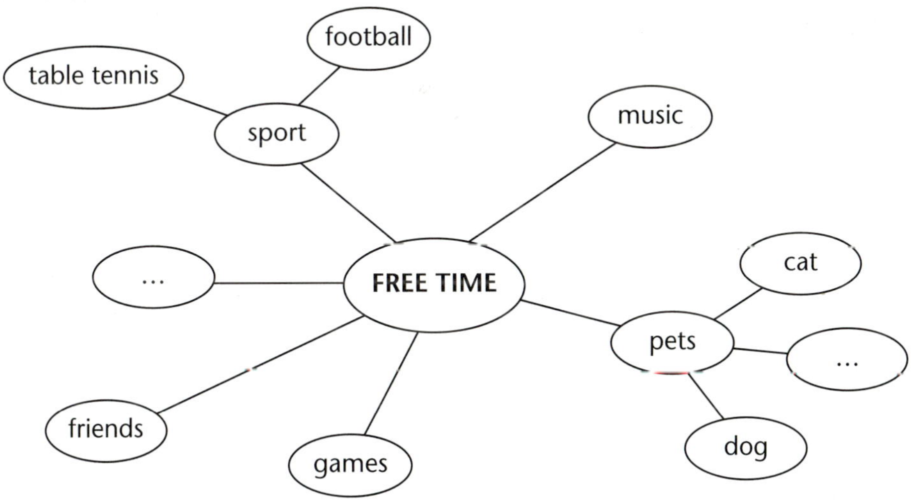

Collect the notices.	**Sammle** die Notizen.
Hang the notice on a noticeboard.	**Hänge** die Notiz an ein schwarzes Brett.
Learn the chant.	**Lerne** den Sprechchor.
Make a **mindmap**/a **class survey**.	Mache ein **Wortnetz**/eine **Umfrage in der Klasse**.
Match the (sentence) **parts.**	**Ordne die** (Satz)**teile zu.**

singer

A2

free time [ˌfriː 'taɪm]	Freizeit	
table tennis ['teɪbl ˌtenɪs]	Tischtennis	
when [wen]	wann	
gym (= gymnasium) [dʒɪm, dʒɪm'neɪziəm]	Turnhalle	
special offer [ˌspeʃl‿'ɒfə]	Sonderangebot	
phone [fəʊn]	Telefon	
singer ['sɪŋə]	Sänger/in	
look for ['lʊk fə]	suchen nach	
new [njuː]	neu	George has a **new** bike.
member ['membə]	Mitglied	
after ['ɑːftə]	nach	I **want to** go shopping **after** school.
on [ɒn]	*hier:* am, an	
for sale [fə 'seɪl]	zu verkaufen	
size [saɪz]	Größe	When is the next match? – **On** Friday.
year [jɪə]	Jahr; *hier:* Schuljahr	
kitten ['kɪtn]	Kätzchen, junge Katze	
home [həʊm]	Zuhause	
next [nekst]	nächste(r, s)	
trip [trɪp]	Ausflug	
Mrs ['mɪsɪz]	Frau *(Anrede)*	Can you **come next** weekend? – Yes, I can.
want [wɒnt]	wünschen; wollen	
meet [miːt]	(sich) treffen	
young [jʌŋ]	jung	
people *(pl)* ['piːpl]	Leute	
other ['ʌðə]	andere(r, s)	
European [jʊərə'piːən]	europäische(r, s)	
country ['kʌntri]	Land	
join [dʒɔɪn]	mitmachen bei; beitreten	
project ['prɒdʒekt]	Projekt	
information *(no pl)* [ˌɪnfə'meɪʃn]	Information	
Mr ['mɪstə]	Herr *(Anrede)*	This is **Mr** Smith. 
contact ['kɒntækt]	Kontakt	
all [ɔːl]	alle(s)	**All** Caroline's new friends like pets.
noticeboard ['nəʊtɪsˌbɔːd]	Aushang, schwarzes Brett	
more [mɔː]	mehr	
cup [kʌp]	Tasse; *hier:* Pokal; Cup	
final ['faɪnl]	Endspiel	

[əʊ] phone, home, noticeboard

	against [ə'genst]	gegen	Hendon School plays **against** Holland Park School.
	where [weə]	wo	
	come [kʌm]	kommen	
	watch [wɒtʃ]	zusehen, zuschauen	
	bring [brɪŋ]	(mit)bringen	Can I **bring** my friends? – Yes, **of course**.
	scarf (*pl* -s *or* scarves) [skɑːf, skɑːvz]	Schal	
	family ['fæmli]	Familie	
	welcome ['welkəm]	willkommen!	
	of course [əv 'kɔːs]	natürlich	
	give [gɪv]	geben	Can you **give** me your pen, please? – Yes, here you are.
	friendly match [ˌfrendli 'mætʃ]	Freundschaftsspiel	
	very ['veri]	sehr	
	funny ['fʌni]	lustig, witzig, komisch	
A3	find out about [faɪnd‿'aʊt‿əˌbaʊt]	sich informieren über	
	place [pleɪs]	Ort; Platz	
	day [deɪ]	Tag	

family

Days of the week

Monday ['mʌndeɪ]	Montag
Tuesday ['tjuːzdeɪ]	Dienstag
Wednesday ['wenzdeɪ]	Mittwoch
Thursday ['θɜːzdeɪ]	Donnerstag
Friday ['fraɪdeɪ]	Freitag
Saturday ['sætədeɪ]	Samstag
Sunday ['sʌndeɪ]	Sonntag

	time [taɪm]	(Uhr)zeit	
A4	**picture** ['pɪktʃə]	Bild	
	answer ['ɑːnsə]	Antwort	
	question ['kwestʃn]	Frage	? **question** ≠ **answer**
	for [fɔː]	für	
	notice ['nəʊtɪs]	Anzeige; Notiz	
	interesting ['ɪntrəstɪŋ]	interessant	
A5	**phone** [fəʊn]	anrufen	
	about [ə'baʊt]	*hier:* wegen	
	What's up? [wɒts‿'ʌp]	Was ist los?	
	now [naʊ]	jetzt	
	tomorrow [tə'mɒrəʊ]	morgen	**When** is the party? – It's **tomorrow**.
	I can't wait. [aɪ ˌkɑːnt 'weɪt]	Ich kann's kaum erwarten.	
	excited [ɪk'saɪtɪd]	aufgeregt, gespannt	
	What's wrong? [wɒts 'rɒŋ]	Was ist denn los?	
	cold [kəʊld]	Erkältung	
	Oh dear. [əʊ 'dɪə]	Du meine Güte!	I have a cold. – **Oh dear. I'm sorry.**
	I'm sorry. [aɪm 'sɒri]	Das tut mir Leid.	

WORDS THEME 3

	run [rʌn]	laufen, rennen
	fast [fɑːst]	schnell
	then [ðen]	dann
	why [waɪ]	warum
	need [niːd]	brauchen
	player ['pleɪə]	Spieler/in
	See you on … ['siː jə‿ˌɒn]	Bis …
A6	**child** (*pl* **children**) [tʃaɪld, 'tʃɪldrən]	Kind
A7	sit [sɪt]	sitzen
	shoe [ʃuː]	Schuh
A8	a lot [ə 'lɒt]	sehr
	wear [weə]	tragen
	sock [sɒk]	Socke
	boot [buːt]	Stiefel
	kit [kɪt]	Trikot
	coach [kəʊtʃ]	Trainer
	goalkeeper ['gəʊlˌkiːpə]	Tormann/Torfrau
	CU (= See you.) ['siː jə]	Bis bald.
A9	put on ['pʊt‿ɒn]	anziehen
	here [hɪə]	hier
	kick [kɪk]	treten, schießen, kicken
	choose [tʃuːz]	auswählen
B1	**It's me.** [ɪts 'miː]	Ich bin's.
B2	**help** [help]	Hilfe
	playing field ['pleɪɪŋ ˌfiːld]	Sportplatz
	sports centre ['spɔːts‿ˌsentə]	Sportcenter
B3	winner ['wɪnə]	Gewinner/in; Sieger/in
	loser ['luːzə]	Verlierer/in
	news *(no pl)* [njuːz]	Nachrichten
	fantastic *(informal)* [fæn'tæstɪk]	fantastisch
	beat [biːt]	schlug/schlugen
	goal [gəʊl]	Tor
	scored [skɔːd]	schoss/schossen
	was [wɒz]	war
	win [wɪn]	gewinnen
	won [wʌn]	gewann/gewannen
	minute ['mɪnɪt]	Minute
	Better luck next year. [ˌbetə lʌk 'nekst jɪə]	Vielleicht klappt es nächstes Jahr besser.
	were [wɜː]	warst/waren/wart
	score [skɔː]	Punktestand; Spielstand
B4	had [hæd]	hatte/hatten
B5	**do** [duː]	machen, tun
	stand [stænd]	stehen

She can **run fast.**

Dein eigenes Bildwörterbuch

Um dir Hauptwörter besser zu merken, kannst du Bilder aus Zeitschriften oder Katalogen ausschneiden, zum Beispiel Möbel, Kleider oder Lebensmittel. Klebe die Bilder auf ein Blatt Papier und schreibe die dazugehörigen Vokabeln direkt an das Bild. Lege das Blatt in deinem Hefter ab. So legst du dein eigenes Bildwörterbuch an.

	a little [ə 'lɪtl]	ein bisschen
	know [nəʊ]	wissen; kennen
	tell [tel]	erzählen
	joke [dʒəʊk]	Witz
	wiggle ['wɪgl]	wackeln mit
	ride [raɪd]	fahren
	unicycle ['juːnɪˌsaɪkl]	Einrad
	press-up ['presʌp]	Liegestütz
	whistle ['wɪsl]	pfeifen
	speak [spiːk]	sprechen

ride a bike

Charlie and Caroline **speak** English.

Languages

English ['ɪnglɪʃ]	Englisch
German ['dʒɜːmən]	Deutsch
Italian [ɪ'tæliən]	Italienisch
Turkish ['tɜːkɪʃ]	Türkisch
Russian [rʌʃn]	Russisch
Polish [pɒlɪʃ]	Polnisch

B6	**answer** ['ɑːnsə]	(be)antworten
	swimming ['swɪmɪŋ]	Schwimmen
	riding ['raɪdɪŋ]	Reiten
	at home [æt 'həʊm]	zu Hause
	horse [hɔːs]	Pferd
	near [nɪə]	nahe
	it's called [ɪts 'kɔːld]	es heißt
C1	**animal** ['ænɪml]	Tier
	pet [pet]	Haustier
	tiger ['taɪgə]	Tiger
	fish [fɪʃ]	Fisch
	spider ['spaɪdə]	Spinne
	hedgehog ['hedʒˌhɒg]	Igel
	crocodile ['krɒkəˌdaɪl]	Krokodil
	live [lɪv]	leben, wohnen
C2	wild [waɪld]	wild
	road [rəʊd]	Straße
	quick [kwɪk]	schnell
	careful ['keəfl]	vorsichtig
	small [smɔːl]	klein
	snail [sneɪl]	Schnecke
	keep [kiːp]	(be)halten, aufbewahren
	flat [flæt]	Wohnung
	put [pʊt]	setzen, stellen, legen
	box [bɒks]	Schachtel
	floor [flɔː]	Boden
	mum *(informal)* [mʌm]	Mama, Mutti
	some [sʌm]	etwas
	take [teɪk]	(mit)nehmen
	back [bæk]	zurück

horse

Goldfish are **small animals**.

Can I **keep** the **hedgehog**?
– No, it's a wild **animal**.

C3	**happy** ['hæpi]	glücklich; zufrieden; fröhlich
	into ['ɪntʊ]	in
C4	elephant ['elɪfənt]	Elefant
	bird [bɜːd]	Vogel
	house [haʊs]	Haus
	basket ['bɑːskɪt]	Korb
	cage [keɪdʒ]	Käfig
C6	**think** [θɪŋk]	(nach)denken, glauben, meinen
C7	dark [dɑːk]	dunkel
	dachshund ['dæksnd]	Dackel
	dream [driːm]	Traum
C8	would [wʊd]	würde
	love [lʌv]	lieben, sehr gern mögen
	ride [raɪd]	*hier:* reiten
	together [tə'geðə]	zusammen, gemeinsam
	best [best]	beste(r, s)
	live [lɪv]	leben, wohnen
	room [ruːm]	Zimmer, Raum
	stable ['steɪbl]	Stall, Box
	carrot ['kærət]	Karotte
C9	count [kaʊnt]	zählen
	least [liːst]	am wenigsten
	walk [wɔːk]	(zu Fuß) gehen
	swim [swɪm]	schwimmen
	fly [flaɪ]	fliegen
O1	°vet [vet]	Tierarzt, Tierärztin
	°so [səʊ]	also
	°hamster ['hæmstə]	Hamster
	°tip [tɪp]	Rat(schlag), Tipp
	°wheel [wiːl]	Rad
	°clean [kliːn]	sauber
	°soft [sɒft]	weich
	°sleep [sliːp]	schlafen
	°make sure [ˌmeɪk 'ʃɔː]	sich versichern, darauf achten
	°fresh [freʃ]	frisch
	°out of ['aʊt‿əv]	aus
	°night [naɪt]	Nacht
	°at night [ət 'naɪt]	nachts
	°safe [seɪf]	sicher
	°wake up [ˌweɪk‿'ʌp]	aufwecken
O2	°understand [ˌʌndə'stænd]	verstehen
	°raccoon [rə'kuːn]	Waschbär/in
	°sanctuary ['sæŋktʃuəri]	Tierpflegestation
	°in the dark [ˌɪn ðə 'dɑːk]	im Dunkeln
	°garden ['gɑːdn]	Garten
	°afternoon [ˌaftə'nuːn]	Nachmittag

happy

My **bird** has a nice **cage**.

cage

ride a bike **ride** a horse

I can't **swim** very fast.

Birds can **fly**.

What animals are they?
[sneɪl] [spaɪdə] [maɪs]
[dogz] [gəʊldfɪʃ] [kæts]

	°worry ['wʌri]	sich Sorgen machen
	°ugly ['ʌgli]	hässlich
	°true [truː]	wahr
	°beetle ['biːtl]	Käfer
	°him [hɪm]	ihm, ihn
O3	°mouse (*pl* mice) [maʊs, maɪs]	Maus
	°rather ['rɑːðə]	ziemlich
	°tail [teɪl]	Schwanz
	°any [eni]	irgendein(e)
	°chin [tʃɪn]	Kinn
	°at all [ət‿'ɔːl]	überhaupt
	°run about [ˌrʌn‿ə'baʊt]	herumrennen
	°nibble ['nɪbl]	knabbern
	°touch [tʌtʃ]	berühren
	°no one ['nəʊ ˌwʌn]	niemand
	°seem [siːm]	scheinen
	°much [mʌtʃ]	viel; sehr
	°rhyming ['raɪmɪŋ]	Reim-
	°own [əʊn]	eigene(r, s)

Schwierige Wörter
Wenn du merkst, dass du bei der Schreibweise einiger englischer Wörter Schwierigkeiten hast, kannst du Folgendes tun: Schreibe das Wort auf einen großen Zettel und markiere die Stelle, die dir die größten Probleme bereitet. Hänge den Zettel in deinem Zimmer auf. Du wirst merken, dass du das Wort bald ganz richtig schreiben kannst!

Wortbilder
Schau dir einmal die Abbildungen der Wörter an. Vielleicht kannst du dir Vokabeln besser merken, wenn du daraus solche „Wortbilder" machst. Versuche es einmal selbst mit den Wörtern *house* und *rain* oder mit Tiernamen. Wer kann das interessanteste oder lustigste Wortbild erfinden?

Theme 4 • The way we live

Say it in English

So kann man …

sagen, dass es sich um eine gute Idee handelt	That's a great idea.
jemanden höflich begrüßen	Nice to meet you.
fragen, wie es jemandem geht – und darauf antworten	How are you? – Fine, thank you.
sagen, dass jemand Recht hat	You're right.
sagen, dass man sich nicht sicher ist	I'm not sure.
über Gewohnheiten sprechen	I often water the plants.

Word field

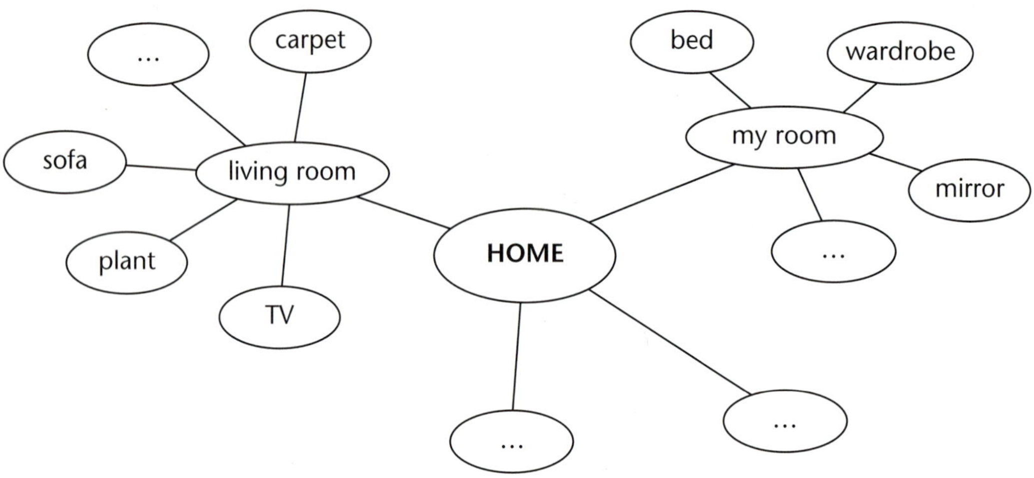

	way [weɪ]	Weg; *hier:* Art und Weise
A1	**room** [ruːm]	Zimmer, Raum
A3	visit ['vɪzɪt]	Besuch
	invite [ɪn'vaɪt]	einladen
	sleepover ['sliːpˌəʊvə]	Übernachtung
	afternoon ['ɑːftəˌnuːn]	Nachmittag
	stay [steɪ]	bleiben
	night [naɪt]	Nacht
	bed [bed]	Bett
	sleep [sliːp]	schlafen
	idea [aɪ'dɪə]	Idee
	What's … like? [wɒts laɪk]	Wie ist …?
	really ['rɪəli]	wirklich
	desk [desk]	Schreibtisch

Charlie's **room** is not very big.

Our cat sometimes **sleeps** on my **bed**.

That's a good **idea**!

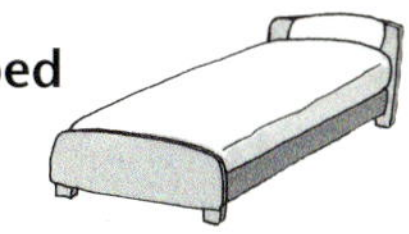
bed

desk

These beginnings/ sentences **can help you.**	**Diese** Anfänge/Sätze **können dir helfen.**
How many people/… **are there?**	**Wie viele** Leute/… **gibt es?**
Work in groups of three/four/…	**Arbeite in** Dreier-/ Vierer-/…**gruppen.**
Start like this: …	**Fang so an:** …
Find out who does what.	**Finde heraus**, wer was tut.

	chair [tʃeə]	Stuhl
	wardrobe ['wɔːdrəʊb]	Kleiderschrank
	under ['ʌndə]	unter
	window ['wɪndəʊ]	Fenster
	shelf (*pl* **shelves**) [ʃelf, ʃelvz]	Regal
	CD player [siː'diː ˌpleɪə]	CD-Player
	chat [tʃæt]	Unterhaltung, Plauderei
	fine [faɪn]	in Ordnung, gut
	station ['steɪʃn]	Bahnhof
	must [mʌst]	müssen
	tidy up [ˌtaɪdi‿'ʌp]	aufräumen
	already [ɔːl'redi]	schon
	just a minute [ˌdʒʌst‿ə 'mɪnɪt]	einen Augenblick/Moment
	forget [fə'get]	vergessen
	homework (*no pl*) ['həʊmˌwɜːk]	Hausaufgaben
A4	uniform ['juːnɪˌfɔːm]	Uniform
	elephant ['elɪfənt]	Elefant
A5	**untidy** [ʌn'taɪdi]	unordentlich
	sock [sɒk]	Socke
	floor [flɔː]	Boden
	look for ['lʊk fə]	suchen nach
	twin [twɪn]	Zwilling, Zwillings-

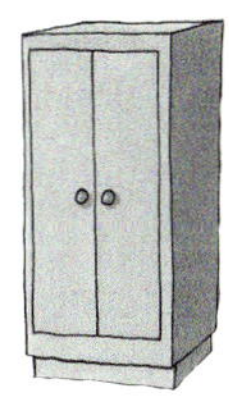
wardrobe

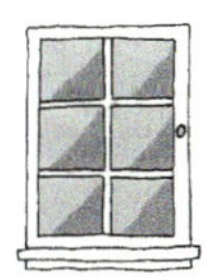
window

shelf

Micky is **under** the cheese.

homework

	brother ['brʌðə]	Bruder	Caroline has one **brother**, George.
	watch out [wɒtʃ‿'aʊt]	aufpassen, sich in Acht nehmen	
	dear … [dɪə]	liebe/r …	
	'cause (= because) [kəz, bɪ'kɒz]	weil, da	
	quite [kwaɪt]	ziemlich	
	It won't take long. [ɪt ˌwəʊnt‿teɪk 'lɒŋ]	Es wird nicht lange dauern.	
	alone [ə'ləʊn]	allein	
	ready ['redi]	fertig	Are you **ready**? – Yes, I am.
	clear [klɪə]	*hier:* aufgeräumt	
A6	**here** [hɪə]	hier	
	keep [kiːp]	*hier:* aufbewahren	
	sports [spɔːts]	Sport	[ɔː] floor, sports, wall
	gear [gɪə]	Ausrüstung, Sachen	
	box [bɒks]	Schachtel	
	wall [wɔːl]	Wand	
B1	busy ['bɪzi]	beschäftigt	
	first [fɜːst]	zuerst; als Erstes	
	do the shopping [ˌduː ðə 'ʃɒpɪŋ]	einkaufen (gehen)	My mum and dad **do the shopping** together.
	cook [kʊk]	kochen	
	delicious [de'lɪʃəs]	köstlich, lecker	
	°moussaka *(no pl)* [muː'sɑːkə]	Moussaka	Caroline's dad can **cook** Moussaka.
	clean [kliːn]	sauber machen; putzen	
	set the table [ˌset ðə 'teɪbl]	den Tisch decken	
	lunch [lʌntʃ]	Mittagessen	
	do the washing up [ˌduː ðə ˌwɒʃɪŋ‿'ʌp]	abspülen	Can you **do the washing up**, please? – No sorry. I'm **hoover**ing the **living room**.
	living room ['lɪvɪŋ ˌruːm]	Wohnzimmer	
	hoover ['huːvə]	staubsaugen	
	carpet ['kɑːpɪt]	Teppich	
	water ['wɔːtə]	gießen	
	plant [plɑːnt]	Pflanze	
	job [dʒɒb]	Arbeit, Tätigkeit	
	watch TV [ˌwɒtʃ tiː'viː]	fernsehen	Can you **set the table**, please?
	TV (= television) [ˌtiː'viː, 'telɪˌvɪʒn]	Fernseher, Fernsehen	
B3	the tube [ðə 'tjuːb]	die (Londoner) U-Bahn	
	way [weɪ]	Weg	
	get on [get‿'ɒn]	einsteigen (in)	
	get off [get‿'ɒf]	aussteigen (aus)	
B4	**hear** [hɪə]	hören	
	almost ['ɔːlməʊst]	fast, beinahe	
	train [treɪn]	Zug	
	meet [miːt]	(sich) treffen	
	exit ['eksɪt]	Ausgang	

cold [kəʊld]	kalt	Is it **cold** in **winter** in England?
some [sʌm]	etwas	
snow [snəʊ]	Schnee	
always ['ɔːlweɪz]	immer	
sell [sel]	verkaufen	
hot [hɒt]	heiß	
chestnut ['tʃesˌnʌt]	Kastanie	
winter ['wɪntə]	Winter	
snowball ['snəʊˌbɔːl]	Schneeball	
poor [pɔː]	arm	
drop [drɒp]	fallen lassen	
bag [bæg]	Tasche	
pick up [pɪk‿'ʌp]	aufheben	
still [stɪl]	(immer) noch	
warm [wɔːm]	warm	
neighbour ['neɪbə]	Nachbar/in	
palace ['pæləs]	Palast	
another [ə'nʌðə]	noch eine(r, s)	
plan [plæn]	Plan	
cinema ['sɪnəmə]	Kino	
youth club ['juːθ ˌklʌb]	Jugendzentrum	
walk [wɔːk]	Spaziergang	
exciting [ɪk'saɪtɪŋ]	aufregend; spannend	
number ['nʌmbə]	Zahl; Ziffer; Nummer	
time [taɪm]	*hier:* Mal	
at all [ət‿'ɔːl]	überhaupt	Snow is not warm **at all**.
be cold [bi 'kəʊld]	frieren	
open ['əʊpən]	öffnen	
door [dɔː]	Tür	
follow ['fɒləʊ]	folgen	
parents ['peərənts]	Eltern	**parents** = mum and dad
people *(pl)* ['piːpl]	Leute	
B5 **family name** ['fæmli ˌneɪm]	Nachname, Familienname	Caroline's **family name** is Perrakis.
first name ['fɜːst ˌneɪm]	Vorname	
Nice to meet you. [ˌnaɪs tə 'miːt jə]	Es freut mich, dich/Sie kennen zu lernen.	
How are you? [haʊ‿'ɑː ˌjʊ]	Wie geht es dir/Ihnen/euch?	
just [dʒʌst]	einfach	
call [kɔːl]	nennen	
me [miː]	mir, mich	
dear [dɪə]	Schatz, Engel	
chocolate *(no pl)* ['tʃɒklət]	Schokolade	
C1 **easy** ['iːzi]	einfach	
life *(pl* **lives)** [laɪv, laɪvz]	Leben	
What's up? [wɒts‿'ʌp]	Was ist los?	
angry ['æŋgri]	verärgert; zornig; wütend	
play a trick on sb [ˌpleɪ‿ə 'trɪk‿ɒn ˌsʌmbədi]	jdm einen Streich spielen	

parents and children

	never ['nevə]	nie(mals)
	only ['əʊnli]	nur
	feed [fiːd]	zu essen geben, füttern
	sometimes ['sʌmtaɪmz]	manchmal
	often ['ɒfn]	oft
	Mother's day ['mʌðəz ˌdeɪ]	Muttertag
	rubbish *(no pl)* ['rʌbɪʃ]	Müll
	yuck *(informal)* [jʌk]	i, igitt
	take out [teɪk‿'aʊt]	hinausbringen
	lazy ['leɪzi]	faul
	normally ['nɔːm(ə)li]	normalerweise
	be right [bi 'raɪt]	Recht haben
	Let's … [lets]	Lass(t) uns …
C3	helper ['helpə]	Helfer/in; Gehilfe
	know [nəʊ]	wissen; kennen
	hard [hɑːd]	hart
	every ['evri]	jede(r, s)
	tired ['taɪəd]	müde
C4	**story** ['stɔːri]	Geschichte, Erzählung
C5	worksheet ['wɜːkˌʃiːt]	Arbeitsblatt
C6	project ['prɒdʒekt]	Projekt
	use [juːz]	benutzen
	dance [dɑːns]	tanzen
	maths *(informal)* [mɑːθs]	Mathe
	car [kɑː]	Auto
	repair [rɪ'peə]	reparieren
	no. (= number) ['nʌmbə]	Nr.
C7	**week** [wiːk]	Woche
	ballet *(no pl)* ['bæleɪ]	Ballett
	drink [drɪŋk]	trinken
	lemonade [ˌlemə'neɪd]	Limonade
	president ['prezɪdənt]	Präsident/in
	article ['ɑːtɪkl]	(Zeitungs)artikel
	magazine [ˌmægə'ziːn]	Zeitschrift, Magazin
	food technology [ˌfuːd tek'nɒlədʒi]	Ernährungslehre
	boring ['bɔːrɪŋ]	langweilig
	go out [gəʊ‿'aʊt]	ausgehen
	stay up late [ˌsteɪ‿ʌp 'leɪt]	lang aufbleiben
C8	canteen [kæn'tiːn]	Kantine
	dancing class ['dɑːnsɪŋ ˌklɑːs]	Tanzunterricht
	dictionary ['dɪkʃənri]	Wörterbuch
	help [help]	Hilfe
C9	chain [tʃeɪn]	Kette

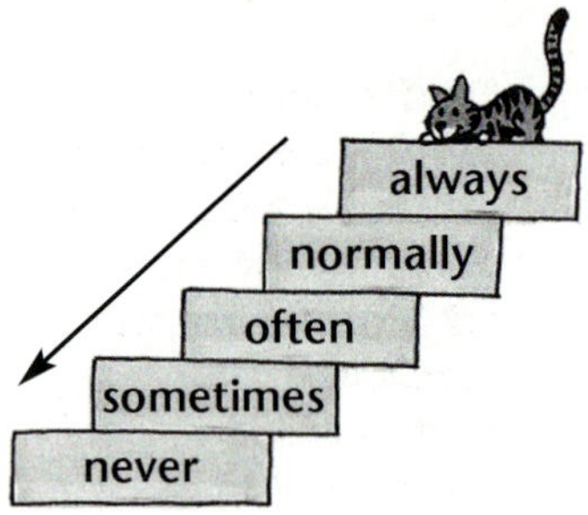

rubbish

The children are **dancing**.

This is our new **car**.

a **week** = seven days

Gillian normally **drinks** tea in the morning.

boring ≠ exciting, interesting

You can look up words in a **dictionary**.

O

°spring [sprɪŋ]	Frühling
°spring-cleaning *(no pl)* [ˌsprɪŋ 'kliːnɪŋ]	Frühjahrsputz
°wipe [waɪp]	abwischen, abputzen
°dust *(no pl)* [dʌst]	Staub
°get [get]	*hier:* hinkommen
°lamp [læmp]	Lampe
°drawer ['drɔːə]	Schublade
°year [jɪə]	Jahr
°lots of ['lɒts‿əv]	viel, jede Menge
°volunteer [ˌvɒlən'tɪə]	Freiwillige/r
°clean [kliːn]	sauber
°in here [ɪn 'hɪə]	hier drin
°throw out [θrəʊ‿'aʊt]	hinauswerfen
°wear [weə]	tragen
°sweep [swiːp]	kehren
°sofa ['səʊfə]	Sofa, Couch
°stool [stuːl]	Hocker
°look [lʊk]	sehen; *hier:* aussehen

Wörter lernen mit dem Computer
Kannst du einen Computer benutzen? Dann kannst du auch so Vokabeln lernen! Lege dir deine persönliche Vokabeldatei an. Dort kannst du alle Wörter hinein schreiben, die du lernen willst. Du kannst deine Wörter auch alphabetisch sortieren lassen und dir so dein eigenes Wörterbuch erstellen.

Die Uhrzeit
In englischsprachigen Ländern wird die Uhrzeit nicht wie bei uns im 24-Stunden-System, sondern meist im 12-Stunden-System angegeben: statt 18 Uhr 30 sagt man dort 6 Uhr 30. Damit man weiß, ob morgens oder nachmittags gemeint ist, schreibt man *am* (lateinisch: *ante meridiem* = vor Mittag) oder *pm* (*post meridiem* – nach Mittag). 16 Uhr 30 heißt also 4:30pm. Der Ausdruck *o'clock* wird nur bei vollen Stunden im 12-Stunden-System verwendet.

Reimwörter
Damit du dir besser merken kannst, wie bestimmte Wörter ausgesprochen werden, suche Reimwörter für sie. Dir wird auffallen, dass die Reimwörter nicht immer dieselbe Schreibweise haben.

What do you do at home?
Say the words.

set the ['teɪbl]
[duː] the washing [ʌp]
['wɔːtə] the plants
[meɪk] the bed
[wɒtʃ] TV

Theme 5 • People I know

Say it in English

So kann man …

sagen, dass man etwas sehr gern mag	I love …
seine Meinung/eine Vermutung äußern	I think geography is a boring subject./ I think Rajiv is happy.
jemandem zum Geburtstag gratulieren	Happy birthday.
sagen, wann man Geburtstag hat	My birthday is on the second of March.
jemandem seine Hilfe anbieten	Can I help you? What can I do for you?
einen Wunsch äußern	I'd like …
Freude und Begeisterung ausdrücken	Super! Great!
sagen, dass sich jemand vorsehen soll	Watch out!

Word field

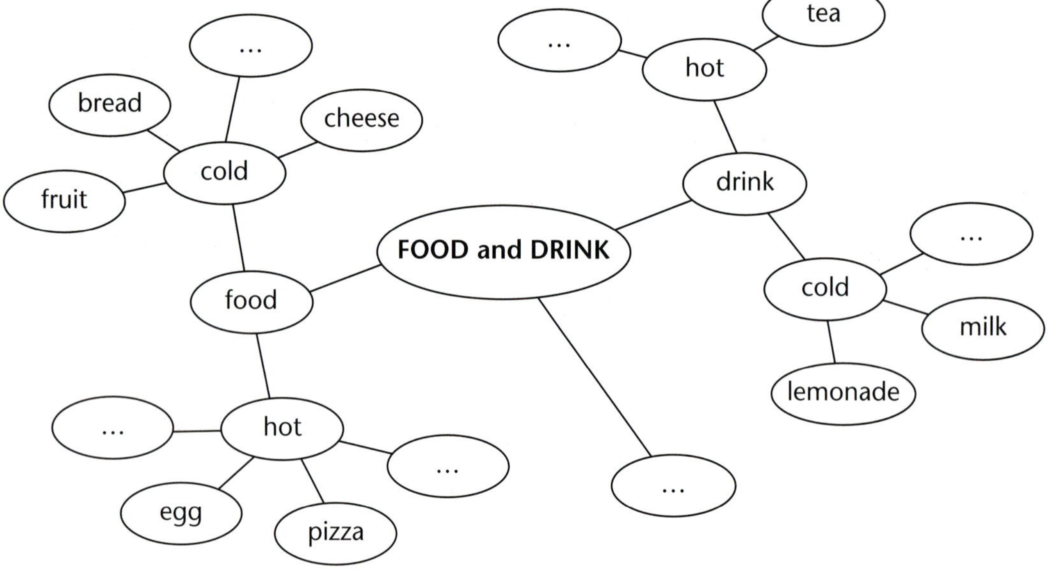

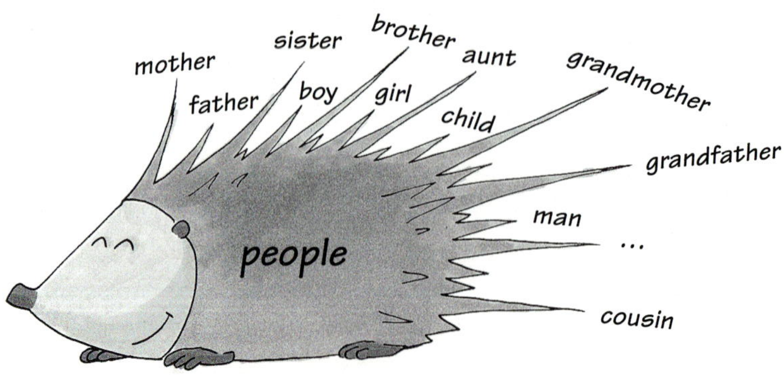

	know [nəʊ]	wissen, kennen	
A3	**last** [lɑːst]	letzte(r, s)	What's your **last lesson** on Friday?
	lesson ['lesn]	Stunde	
	teacher ['tiːtʃə]	Lehrer/in	Our German **teacher** is Frau Weber.
	busy ['bɪzi]	beschäftigt	
	interested ['ɪntrəstɪd]	interessiert	
	love [lʌv]	lieben, sehr gern mögen	I **love** my dog.
	dream [driːm]	träumen	

Compare Rajiv's timetable **with** your timetable.	**Vergleiche** Rajivs Stundenplan **mit** deinem Stundenplan.
Put the scenes in the **correct order.**	Bringe die Szenen in die **richtige Reihenfolge.**
What do you notice?	**Was fällt dir auf?**

	today [tə'deɪ]	heute	**Today** is Tuesday, tomorrow is Wednesday.
	fun *(no pl)* [fʌn]	Spaß	
	invitation [ˌɪnvɪ'teɪʃn]	Einladung	
	birthday ['bɜːθdeɪ]	Geburtstag	Today is his first **birthday**.
	perhaps [pə'hæps]	vielleicht	
	smile [smaɪl]	lächeln	
	go [gəʊ]	gehen; *hier:* werden	
	Sir [sɜː]	Herr *(Anrede)*	
	bell [bel]	Glocke	
	ring [rɪŋ]	klingeln, läuten	
	pupil ['pjuːpl]	Schüler/in	Charlie and Rajiv are **pupils**. They go to Holland Park School.
	jump up [dʒʌmp‿'ʌp]	aufspringen, hochspringen	
	class [klɑːs]	*hier:* Unterricht	
	leave [liːv]	verlassen	
	feel [fiːl]	(sich) fühlen	
	bored [bɔːd]	gelangweilt	**bored** ≠ interested
	unhappy [ʌn'hæpi]	unglücklich	
A4	close [kləʊs]	schließen, zumachen	
A5	**timetable** ['taɪmteɪbl]	Stundenplan	
	registration [ˌredʒɪ'streɪʃn]	Anmeldung	
	assembly [ə'sembli]	Versammlung	
	break [breɪk]	Pause	I always eat an apple in the **break**.
	art [ɑːt]	Kunst	
	science *(no pl)* ['saɪəns]	(Natur)wissenschaft	
	physical education *(no pl)* [ˌfɪzɪkl‿edjʊ'keɪʃn]	Sport(unterricht)	[aɪ] smile, timetable, science
	design and technology [dɪˌzaɪn‿ənd tek'nɒlədʒi]	*erweiterter Werkunterricht*	
	French [frentʃ]	Franzose/Französin; französisch; *hier:* Französisch	

	information and communication technology [ɪnfəˌmeɪʃn‿ənd kəmjuːnɪˌkeɪʃn tek'nɒlədʒi]	Informatik	
	geography [dʒiː'ɒgrəfi]	Erdkunde, Geografie	
	history ['hɪst(ə)ri]	Geschichte	
	religious education [rəˌlɪdʒəs‿edjʊ'keɪʃn]	Religionslehre	
	food technology [ˌfuːd tek'nɒlədʒi]	Ernährungslehre	What time does the film **start**? – At 8:30.
	start [stɑːt]	anfangen	
	interesting ['ɪntrəstɪŋ]	interessant	
	difficult ['dɪfɪklt]	schwierig, schwer	**difficult** = not easy
	subject ['sʌbdʒɪkt]	(Schul)fach	
A6	**every** ['evri]	jede(r, s)	What's your favourite **subject**? – Art.
A7	minute ['mɪnɪt]	Minute	
A9	get up [get‿'ʌp]	aufstehen	
	past [pɑːst]	nach	
	dress [dres]	sich anziehen	
	bacon ['beɪkən]	(Schinken)speck	
	before [bɪ'fɔː]	bevor	**before** ≠ after
	be over [bi‿'əʊvə]	vorbei/aus sein	
	safe [seɪf]	sicher	Can we watch the show? – No, sorry. **It's over**.
	inside [ɪn'saɪd]	innen; *hier:* im Inneren	
	brush [brʌʃ]	(ab)bürsten	
	till [tɪl]	bis	
	shine [ʃaɪn]	scheinen; glänzen, leuchten	

Wörter malen
Manche Wörter lassen sich besser merken, wenn du kleine Bilder dazu malst. Auf diesen Seiten findest du einige lustige Zeichnungen zu englischen Vokabeln. Versuche doch mal, dir selbst welche einfallen zu lassen.

Ordinal Numbers

1st	**first** [fɜːst]	21st	twenty-first [ˌtwenti'fɜːst]
2nd	**second** ['sekənd]	22nd	twenty-second [ˌtwenti'sekənd]
3rd	**third** [θɜːd]	23rd	twenty-third [ˌtwenti'θɜːd]
4th	fourth [fɔːθ]	24th	twenty-fourth [ˌtwenti'fɔːθ]
5th	fifth [fɪfθ]	25th	twenty-fifth [ˌtwenti'fɪfθ]
6th	sixth [sɪksθ]	26th	twenty-sixth [ˌtwenti'sɪksθ]
7th	seventh ['sevnθ]	27th	twenty-seventh [ˌtwenti'sevnθ]
8th	eighth [eɪtθ]	28th	twenty-eighth [ˌtwenti'eɪtθ]
9th	ninth [naɪnθ]	29th	twenty-ninth [ˌtwenti'naɪnθ]
10th	tenth [tenθ]	30th	thirtieth ['θɜːtiəθ]
11th	eleventh [ɪ'levnθ]	31st	thirty-first [ˌθɜːti'fɜːst]
12th	twelfth [twelfθ]		
13th	thirteenth [ˌθɜː'tiːnθ]		
14th	fourteenth [ˌfɔː'tiːnθ]		
15th	fifteenth [ˌfɪf'tiːnθ]		
16th	sixteenth [ˌsɪks'tiːnθ]		
17th	seventeenth [ˌsevn'tiːnθ]		
18th	eighteenth [ˌeɪ'tiːnθ]		
19th	nineteenth [ˌnaɪn'tiːnθ]		
20th	twentieth ['twentiəθ]		

second, first, third
(2nd, 1st, 3rd)

B1	date [deɪt]	Datum	
	Happy birthday [ˌhæpi ˈbɜːθdeɪ]	Alles Gute zum Geburtstag	**Happy birthday!**

Months	**Monate**
January [ˈdʒænjuəri]	Januar
February [ˈfebruəri]	Februar
March [mɑːtʃ]	März
April [ˈeɪprəl]	April
May [meɪ]	Mai
June [dʒuːn]	Juni
July [dʒʊˈlaɪ]	Juli
August [ˈɔːgʌst]	August
September [sepˈtembə]	September
October [ɒkˈtəʊbə]	Oktober
November [nəʊˈvembə]	November
December [dɪˈsembə]	Dezember

mother **father**

B2	calendar [ˈkæləndə]	Kalender	
B3	**aunt** [ɑːnt]	Tante	
	father [ˈfɑːðə]	Vater	dad = **father**
	end [end]	Ende, Schluss	
	tongue twister [ˈtʌŋ ˌtwɪstə]	Zungenbrecher	
B4	**present** [ˈpreznt]	Geschenk	This is mum's birthday **present**.
B5	along [əˈlɒŋ]	entlang	
	weekend [ˌwiːkˈend]	Wochenende	Saturday + Sunday = **weekend**
	noisy [ˈnɔɪzi]	laut	
	fruit [fruːt]	Obst	Apples, oranges and bananas are **fruit**.
	stall [stɔːl]	(Verkaufs)stand	
	melon [ˈmelən]	Melone	
	sell [sel]	verkaufen	**sell** ≠ buy
	sold out [səʊld‿ˈaʊt]	ausverkauft	
	those (*pl of* **that**) [ðəʊz]	diese; jene	
	lovely [ˈlʌvli]	schön, hübsch	You look **lovely** today! – Thank you.
	orange [ˈɒrɪndʒ]	Orange	
	banana [bəˈnɑːnə]	Banane	
	dear [dɪə]	Schatz, Engel	
	walk past [wɔːk ˈpɑːst]	vorbeigehen	
	cap [kæp]	Mütze, Kappe	
	sock [sɒk]	Socke	
	really [ˈrɪəli]	wirklich	
	walk on [wɔk‿ˈɒn]	weitergehen	
	potato (*pl* **-es**) [pəˈteɪtəʊ, pəˈteɪtəʊz]	Kartoffel	
	carrot [ˈkærət]	Karotte	
	cucumber [ˈkjuːˌkʌmbə]	(Salat)gurke	

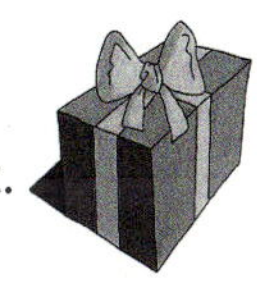

	vegetable ['vedʒtəbl]	Gemüse	**Potatoes**, **carrots** and **tomatoes** are **vegetables**.
	Excuse me! [ɪks'kjuːz ˌmi]	Entschuldigen Sie bitte!, Entschuldigung	
	get through [get 'θruː]	durchgehen, durchkommen	
	tomato (*pl* **-es**) [tə'mɑːtəʊ, tə'mɑːtəʊz]	Tomate	
	just [dʒʌst]	*hier:* nur	
	best [best]	am besten; *hier:* am meisten	
	fantastic *(informal)* [fæn'tæstɪk]	fantastisch	
	perfect ['pɜːfɪkt]	vollkommen, perfekt	
	change [tʃeɪndʒ]	Wechselgeld	
	Christmas ['krɪsməs]	Weihnachten	
B8	**price** [praɪs]	Preis	
	buyer ['baɪə]	Käufer/in	
	seller ['selə]	Verkäufer/in	
C1	preparation [ˌprepə'reɪʃn]	Vorbereitung	
	already [ɔːl'redi]	schon	
	be in a hurry [ˌbi‿ɪn‿ə 'hʌri]	es eilig haben, in Eile sein	
	grandma ['grænˌmɑː]	Oma, Omi	
	prepare [prɪ'peə]	vorbereiten	
	decorate ['dekəˌreɪt]	schmücken	
	uncle ['ʌŋkl]	Onkel	My **uncle** and **aunt** live in Berlin.
	try out [traɪ‿'aʊt]	ausprobieren, testen	
	take a photo [teɪk‿ə 'fəʊtəʊ]	ein Foto machen	She likes to **take photos** of the family.
	camera ['kæm(ə)rə]	Kamera, Fotoapparat	
	carry ['kæri]	tragen	
	glass [glɑːs]	Glas	
	decoration [ˌdekə'reɪʃn]	Dekoration	
	stop [stɒp]	aufhören, beenden	
	cut [kʌt]	schneiden	
	cry [kraɪ]	weinen	
C2	**guest** [gest]	Gast	Gillian, Caroline, Charlie, Rajiv and Emma are David's **guests**.
	use [juːz]	benutzen	
	blow out [bləʊ‿'aʊt]	ausblasen	
	candle ['kændl]	Kerze	
	open ['əʊpən]	öffnen	
	dance [dɑːns]	Tanz	
	person ['pɜːsn]	Person, Mensch	The **year** starts in **January**.
C4	family tree ['fæmli ˌtriː]	Familienstammbaum	
	year [jɪə]	Jahr	
	daughter ['dɔːtə]	Tochter	
	son [sʌn]	Sohn	
	grandmother ['grænˌmʌðə]	Großmutter	

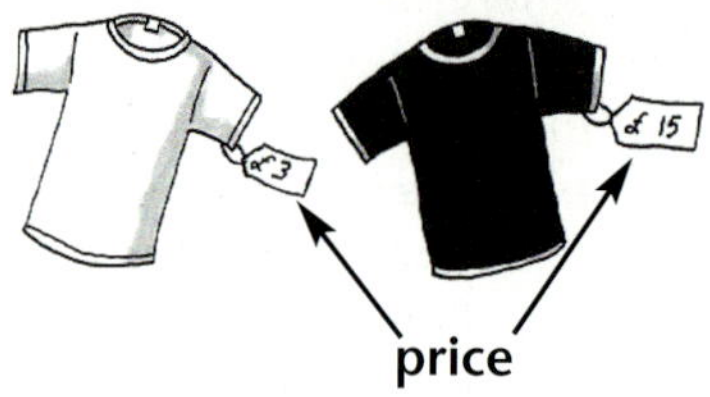

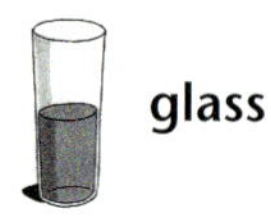

grandfather ['græn,fɑːðə]	Großvater
granddaughter ['græn,dɔːtə]	Enkelin
grandson ['græn,sʌn]	Enkel
wife (*pl* wives) [waɪf, waɪvz]	Ehefrau
husband ['hʌzbənd]	Ehemann
niece [niːs]	Nichte
nephew ['nefjuː]	Neffe
single parent [,sɪŋgl 'peərənt]	Alleinerziehende/r
married ['mærɪd]	verheiratet
divorced [dɪ'vɔːst]	geschieden
C5 **whose** [huːz]	wessen
letter ['letə]	Buchstabe
C6 fantasy ['fæntəsi]	Fantasie
O °brochure ['brəʊʃə]	Broschüre
°plan [plæn]	planen
°information (*no pl*) [,ɪnfə'meɪʃn]	Information
°paper ['peɪpə]	Papier
°colouring pencil [,kʌlərɪŋ 'pensl]	Buntstift
°check [tʃek]	überprüfen, kontrollieren

Vergiss es einfach!
Hast du manchmal Probleme, dir bestimmte Wörter zu merken? Sind es immer wieder dieselben Vokabeln, die dir nicht einfallen? Dann probier es doch mal mit Vergessen!
Das geht so: Suche fünf oder sechs schwierige Wörter aus, die du unbedingt vergessen willst. Schreibe sie auf Zettel und hänge sie neben dein Bett, über deinen Schreibtisch oder an den Badezimmerspiegel. Lies sie bei jeder Gelegenheit durch, damit du dich daran erinnerst, welche Wörter du unbedingt vergessen willst.

Für gute Zuhörer
Du kannst dir Vokabeln auch merken, indem du sie dir immer wieder anhörst. Das funktioniert super! Nimm das englische Wort auf, das du lernen willst – aber vergiss die deutsche Übersetzung nicht! Höre dir die Wörter regelmäßig an, und du wirst bald feststellen, dass du sie gelernt hast.

Which month is it?
[dɪ'sembə]
[dʒuːn]
[sep'tembə]
['ɔːgʌst]
['dʒænjuəri]

Theme 6 • Out and about

Say it in English

So kann man …

sagen, wofür man sich interessiert	I'm interested in maths.
sagen, was man gut kann	I'm good at music.
eine Bestellung aufgeben	A chocolate ice cream, please./ I'd like …, please.
nach Vorlieben fragen	What is your favourite …?
fragen, wo sich etwas befindet	Where is …?
fragen, wann etwas statt findet	When is it …?
fragen, worum es bei einer Sache geht	What is … about?
nach einer Person fragen	Who's that girl?
fragen, was los ist	What's going on?/What's on?/ What's up?/What's wrong?
über das Wetter reden	It's sunny/cloudy/stormy/windy/rainy/foggy. It's hot/warm/cold.

Word field

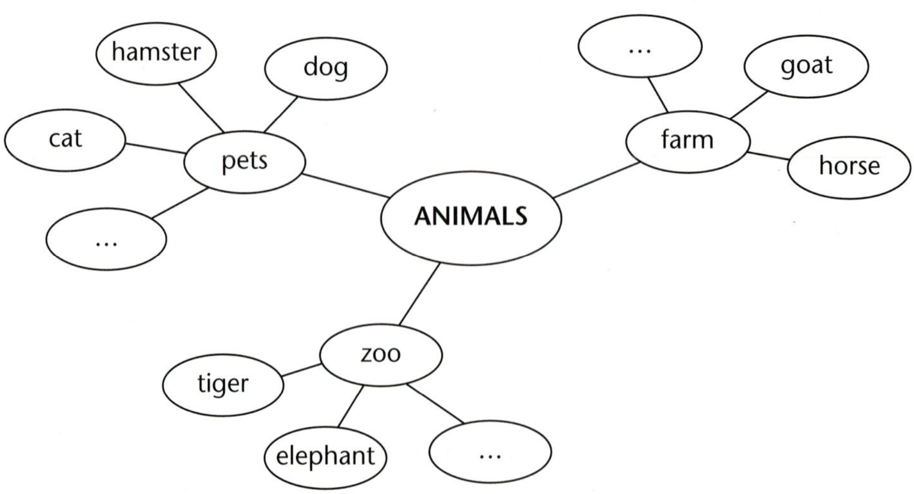

	out and about [ˌaʊt‿ənd‿ə'baʊt]	unterwegs
A1	**be interested in** [bi‿'ɪntrəstɪd‿ɪn]	sich interessieren für
A2	something ['sʌmθɪŋ]	etwas
	competition [ˌkɒmpə'tɪʃn]	Wettbewerb
	own [əʊn]	eigene(r, s)
	move [muːv]	Bewegung
	member ['membə]	Mitglied
	stage [steɪdʒ]	Bühne
	watch [wɒtʃ]	zusehen, zuschauen; *hier:* ansehen
	like [laɪk]	wie
	star [stɑː]	Stern
	planet ['plænɪt]	Planet
	visit ['vɪzɪt]	besuchen
	space *(no pl)* [speɪs]	*hier:* Weltraum
	work *(no pl)* [wɜːk]	Arbeit
	skating *(no pl)* ['skeɪtɪŋ]	Rollerskaten
	practise ['præktɪs]	üben
	show [ʃəʊ]	zeigen
	take part (in) [ˌteɪk 'pɑːt]	teilnehmen (an)
	outing ['aʊtɪŋ]	Ausflug
	farm [fɑːm]	Bauernhof
	tractor ['træktə]	Traktor
	milk [mɪlk]	melken
	cow [kaʊ]	Kuh
	report [rɪ'pɔːt]	Bericht
	newspaper ['njuːzˌpeɪpə]	Zeitung
	reporter [rɪ'pɔːtə]	Reporter/in
	interview ['ɪntəˌvjuː]	befragen
	article ['ɑːtɪkl]	(Zeitungs)artikel
	drama ['drɑːmə]	Theater
	detective story [dɪ'tektɪv ˌstɔːri]	Kriminalroman; Detektivgeschichte
	play [pleɪ]	Spiel; *hier:* (Theater)stück
	knife (*pl* **knives**) [naɪf, naɪvz]	Messer
	sightseeing *(no pl)* ['saɪtˌsiːɪŋ]	Besichtigungen, Sightseeing
	trip [trɪp]	Ausflug
	deep-sea [ˌdiːp'siː]	Tiefsee-
	museum [mjuː'ziːəm]	Museum
	which [wɪtʃ]	welche(r, s)
	sound [saʊnd]	klingen, sich anhören
A3	**guitar** [gɪ'tɑː]	Gitarre
	interest ['ɪntrəst]	Interesse
	president ['prezɪdənt]	Präsident/in
	telescope ['telɪˌskəʊp]	Teleskop
B1	**hungry** ['hʌŋgri]	hungrig
	smell [smel]	Geruch; Duft; Gestank
	pig [pɪg]	Schwein

He sings **like** a real pop star.

star

[w]	<u>w</u>ife, <u>w</u>atch
[v]	<u>v</u>isit, mo<u>v</u>e

cow

Cows and **pigs** are farm animals.

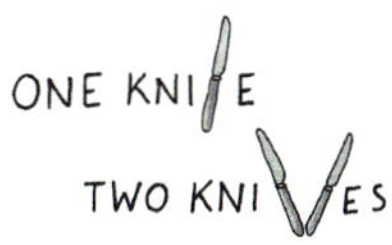

He is **hungry**.

pig

	everywhere ['evriweə]	überall
	beautiful ['bjuːtəfl]	schön
	riding *(no pl)* ['raɪdɪŋ]	Reiten
	sign [saɪn]	(Straßen-/Verkehrs)schild
	half past (three) [ˌhɑːf pɑːst ('θriː)]	halb (vier) (Uhr)
	snack bar ['snæk ˌbɑː]	Imbissstube
	toilet ['tɔɪlət]	Toilette, Klo
	stamp [stæmp]	Briefmarke
	sheep (*pl* **sheep**) [ʃiːp]	Schaf
	goat [gəʊt]	Ziege
	lamb [læm]	Lamm
	out [aʊt]	draußen
	all winter [ˌɔːl 'wɪntə]	den ganzen Winter
	stay [steɪ]	bleiben
	outside [ˌaʊt'saɪd]	im Freien, draußen
	What's going on? [ˌwɒts gəʊɪŋ‿'ɒn]	Was ist los?
	rucksack ['rʌkˌsæk]	Rucksack
	bite [baɪt]	beißen
	worry ['wʌri]	sich Sorgen machen
	bull [bʊl]	Stier, Bulle
B2	point [pɔɪnt]	Stelle, Punkt
	piglet ['pɪglət]	Ferkel
	barn [bɑːn]	Scheune
	tree [triː]	Baum
	go on [gəʊ‿'ɒn]	weitergehen
	turn [tɜːn]	abbiegen
	left [left]	(nach) links
	over ['əʊvə]	über
	bridge [brɪdʒ]	Brücke
B3	**goose** (*pl* **geese**) [guːs, giːs]	Gans
	grass (*pl* -es) [grɑːs, grɑːsɪz]	Gras
	graze [greɪz]	grasen, weiden
B4	**rain** [reɪn]	regnen
	get [get]	*hier:* werden
	wet [wet]	nass
	ice cream [ˌaɪs 'kriːm]	Eiskrem, Eis
	vanilla *(no pl)* [və'nɪlə]	Vanille
	chocolate *(no pl)* ['tʃɒklət]	Schokolade
	strawberry ['strɔːb(ə)ri]	Erdbeere
	lemonade [ˌlemə'neɪd]	Limonade
	mineral water ['mɪn(ə)rəl ˌwɔːtə]	Mineralwasser
	bar [bɑː]	Riegel
	scone [skəʊn]	*brötchenartiges Gebäck*
	no [nəʊ]	kein(e)
	I'll have [aɪl 'hæv]	ich hätte gern
B5	**rain** [reɪn]	Regen
	away [ə'weɪ]	weg
	postcard ['pəʊstˌkɑːd]	Postkarte

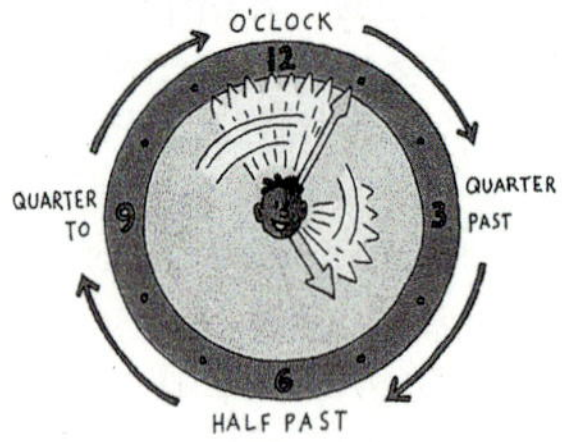

Where's the **toilet**, please?
– It's over there.

lamb = small sheep

stamp

piglet = young pig

goose →

Oh, no! It's **rain**ing again!

ice cream

I'm so hungry! – Here, have some chocolate.

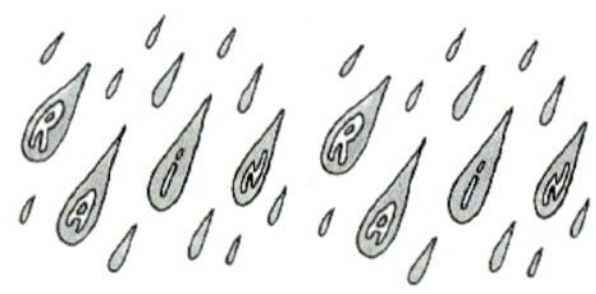

	weather ['weðə]	Wetter
	rainy ['reɪni]	regnerisch
	stormy ['stɔːmi]	stürmisch
	cloudy ['klaʊdi]	bewölkt, bedeckt
	sunny ['sʌni]	sonnig
	snowy ['snəʊi]	schneereich
	windy ['wɪndi]	windig
	foggy ['fɒgi]	neblig
	yesterday ['jestədeɪ]	gestern
	zoo [zuː]	Zoo
	fantastic *(informal)* [fæn'tæstɪk]	fantastisch
	terrible ['terəbl]	schrecklich, furchtbar
	yours [jɔːz]	deine(r, s), Ihre(r, s)
B6	**duck** [dʌk]	Ente
	cock [kɒk]	Hahn
	curly ['kɜːli]	*hier:* Ringel-
	tail [teɪl]	Schwanz
	minute ['mɪnɪt]	Minute
	for now [fə 'naʊ]	fürs Erste
C1	theatre ['θɪətə]	Theater
	shark (*pl* -s *or* -) [ʃɑːk, ʃɑːks]	Hai(fisch)
	murderer ['mɜːdərə]	Mörder/in
	open day ['əʊpən ˌdeɪ]	Tag der offenen Tür
C2	talk [tɔːk]	Gespräch; Unterhaltung
	really ['rɪəli]	wirklich
	fall [fɔːl]	fallen
C3	cowgirl ['kaʊˌgɜːl]	Cowgirl
	bullfighter ['bʊlˌfaɪtə]	Stierkämpfer/in
	ride (on) [raɪd]	Fahrt (mit)
	farmer ['fɑːmə]	Bauer/Bäuerin, Farmer/in
	poor [pɔː]	arm
	exciting [ɪk'saɪtɪŋ]	aufregend; spannend
	very much [ˌveri 'mʌtʃ]	sehr
	in the end [ˌɪn ðiː‿'end]	letzten Endes
C4	**What is ... about?** [ˌwɒt‿ɪz ə'baʊt]	Worum geht es in/bei ...?
	performance [pə'fɔːməns]	Vorführung
	main hall [meɪn 'hɔːl]	Haupthalle
	exhibition [ˌeksɪ'bɪʃn]	Ausstellung
	fact [fækt]	Tatsache
	sun [sʌn]	Sonne
	moon [muːn]	Mond
	expert ['ekspɜːt]	Experte/Expertin
	through [θruː]	durch
	track [træk]	*hier:* Anlage
	underwater [ˌʌndə'wɔːtə]	Unterwasser-
	bull-riding ['bʊlˌraɪdɪŋ]	Bullenreiten
	contest ['kɒntest]	Wettbewerb
	special edition [ˌspeʃl‿ɪ'dɪʃn]	Sonderausgabe
	fascinating ['fæsɪneɪtɪŋ]	faszinierend
	money *(no pl)* ['mʌni]	Geld

sunny

windy

yesterday – today – tomorrow

shark

What is the story **about**? – It's about pets.

sun

Read the words and say them.

[dʌk]	['taɪgə]	[bɜːd]
[kæt]	[pɪg]	[ʃiːp]
[dɒg]	[hɔːs]	[bʊl]
[guːs]	['hedʒˌhɒg]	

I don't have **money** for an ice cream.

	charity ['tʃærəti]	wohltätiger Zweck
	the same [ðə 'seɪm]	der-/die-/dasselbe
C5	What's on? [wɒts‿'ɒn]	Was gibt's?
O	°scene [siːn]	Szene; *hier:* Schauplatz
	°library ['laɪbrəri]	Bibliothek, Bücherei
	°enter ['entə]	Auftritt
	°Dr (= Doctor) ['dɒktə]	Dr.
	°go out [gəʊ‿'aʊt]	(hinaus)gehen
	°cook [kʊk]	Koch/Köchin
	°never know a thing [ˌnevə ˌnəʊ‿ə 'θɪŋ]	nie irgendwas wissen
	°exit ['eksɪt]	Ausgang; *hier:* Abgang
	°cinema ['sɪnəmə]	Kino
	°wonderful ['wʌndəfl]	wunderbar, wundervoll
	°onto ['ɒntə]	auf
	°detective [dɪ'tektɪv]	Kriminalbeamte/r; (Privat)detektiv/in
	°calm down [kɑːm 'daʊn]	sich beruhigen
	°let [let]	lassen
	°dead [ded]	tot
	°police *(npl)* [pə'liːs]	Polizei
	°kill [kɪl]	töten
	°sit down [sɪt 'daʊn]	sich (hin)setzen
	°now then ['naʊ ðen]	also
	°have lunch [həv 'lʌntʃ]	zu Mittag essen
	°because [bɪ'kɒz]	weil
	°only ['əʊnli]	einzige(r, s)
	°have got [həv 'gɒt]	haben
	°Come on! [kʌm‿'ɒn]	Komm jetzt!, Mach schon!
	°curtain ['kɜːtən]	Vorhang
	°pen pal ['pen ˌpæl]	Brieffreund/in
	°world [wɜːld]	Welt
	°female ['fiːmeɪl]	weiblich
	°male [meɪl]	männlich
	°country ['kʌntri]	Land
	°look for ['lʊk fə]	suchen nach
	°real [rɪəl]	wirklich
	°around [ə'raʊnd]	um
	°hazel ['heɪzl]	haselnussbraun
	°sort of ['sɔːt‿əv]	so 'ne Art von
	°wanna (= want to) ['wɒnə]	*hier:* willst du
	°chat [tʃæt]	plaudern; sich unterhalten; chatten
	°C ya. (= See you.) ['siː jə]	Bis bald.
	°drums *(pl)* [drʌmz]	Schlagzeug
	°try [traɪ]	versuchen, probieren
	°language ['læŋgwɪdʒ]	Sprache
	°sad [sæd]	traurig
	°joking ['dʒəʊkɪŋ]	scherzhaft; *hier:* scherzend
	°shocked [ʃɒkt]	schockiert, entsetzt
	°kiss [kɪs]	Kuss
	°hug [hʌg]	Umarmung

Vokabel-Memory
Spielst du gerne Memory? Dann spiele doch mal Vokabel-Memory mit einem Freund oder einer Freundin. Das geht so: Jeder schreibt acht englische Wörter auf kleine Kärtchen. Dann schreibt ihr die Übersetzungen der Wörter auf acht weitere Kärtchen. Und dann geht's los: Legt eure Karten verdeckt aus und fangt an. Wer hat die meisten Wortpaare gefunden?

Vokabel-Domino
Für das Vokabel-Domino benötigst du eine/n Partner/in. Du beginnst das Spiel, indem du eine englische Vokabel waagerecht auf ein leeres Blatt Papier schreibst. Nun muss dein/e Partner/in die deutsche Bedeutung deines Wortes nennen. Bei einer richtigen Antwort gibt's einen Punkt und er/sie ist an der Reihe, ein englisches Wort „anzulegen". Viel Spaß!

A

a/an [ə,ən] ein(e) 1/I
about [ə'baʊt] über 1/A3
about [ə'baʊt] wegen 3/A5
out and about [ˌaʊt‿ənd‿ə'baʊt] unterwegs 6/I
What about …? *(informal)* [ˌwɒt‿ə'baʊt] Was ist mit …?, Wie wäre es mit …? 1/I
What is … about? [ˌwɒt‿ɪz ə'baʊt] Worum geht es in/bei …? 6/C4
Act the scene. [ˌækt ðə 'siːn] Spiele die Szene nach. 2/A2
add [æd] hinzufügen 2/C5
after ['ɑːftə] nach 3/A2
afternoon ['ɑːftəˌnuːn] Nachmittag 4/A3
again [ə'gen] wieder; noch einmal 5/A8
against [ə'genst] gegen 3/A2
all [ɔːl] ganz, völlig 2/A5; alle(s) 3/A2
almost ['ɔːlməʊst] fast, beinahe 4/B4
alone [ə'ləʊn] allein 4/A5
along [ə'lɒŋ] entlang 5/B5
alphabetical [ˌælfə'betɪkl] alphabetisch 2/A5
already [ɔːl'redi] schon 1/A8
always ['ɔːlweɪz] immer 4/B4
and [ənd] und 1/I
angry ['æŋgri] verärgert; zornig; wütend 4/C1
animal ['ænɪml] Tier 3/C1
another [ə'nʌðə] noch eine(r, s) 2/A4
answer ['ɑːnsə] Antwort 3/A4
answer ['ɑːnsə] (be)antworten 3/B6
° any [eni] irgendein(e) 3/O3
any more [ˌeni 'mɔː] nicht mehr 1/B7
Anything else? [ˌeniθɪŋ‿'els] Darf es noch etwas sein? 2/C6
apple ['æpl] Apfel 1/A5
April ['eɪprəl] April 5/B1
aquarium (*pl* -s *or* -ria) [ə'kweəriəm, ə'kweəriəmz, ə'kweəriə] Aquarium 3/C4
arm [ɑːm] Arm 2/A4
° around [ə'raʊnd] um 6/O
art [ɑːt] Kunst 5/A5
article ['ɑːtɪkl] (Zeitungs)artikel 4/C7
ask [ɑːsk] fragen; bitten 1/B9
assembly [ə'sembli] Versammlung 5/A5
at [æt] auf, an, in, bei 1/B2
at all [ət‿'ɔːl] überhaupt 4/B4
at home [æt 'həʊm] zu Hause 3/B6
° at night [ət 'naɪt] nachts 3/O1
August ['ɔːgʌst] August 5/C1
aunt [ɑːnt] Tante 5/B3
away [ə'weɪ] weg 2/A5

B

back [bæk] Rücken 2/A4; Rückseite 5/B8
back [bæk] zurück 1/A8
bacon ['beɪkən] (Schinken)speck 2/B2
bag [bæg] Tasche 4/B4
° bake [beɪk] backen 2/B6
baked beans [ˌbeɪkt 'biːnz] Baked Beans *(Bohnen in Tomatensauce)* 2/B2
at the baker's [ˌæt ðə 'beɪkəz] in der Bäckerei, beim Bäcker 2/C6
ball [bɔːl] Ball 3/A9
ballet *(no pl)* ['bæleɪ] Ballett 4/C7
banana [bə'nɑːnə] Banane 5/B5
bar [bɑː] Riegel 6/B4
barn [bɑːn] Scheune 6/B2
basket ['bɑːskɪt] Korb 3/C4
basketball ['bɑːskɪtˌbɔːl] Basketball 3/B6
bathroom ['bɑːθˌruːm] Bad(ezimmer) 2/A2
be [biː] sein 1/I
beat [biːt] verrühren 2/B6; schlagen; schlug/schlugen 3/B3
beautiful ['bjuːtəfl] schön 6/B1
because [bɪ'kɒz] weil 1/A8
bed [bed] Bett 4/A3
° beetle ['biːtl] Käfer 3/O2
before [bɪ'fɔː] bevor 1/B2; vor 2/B4
beginning [bɪ'gɪnɪŋ] Anfang 4/A6
behind [bɪ'haɪnd] hinter 2/A2
bell [bel] Glocke 5/A3
best [best] beste(r, s) 3/C8; am besten; am meisten 5/B5
better ['betə] besser 6/C3
big [bɪg] groß 2/A6
bike [baɪk] (Fahr)rad 1/B5
bird [bɜːd] Vogel 3/C4
birthday ['bɜːθdeɪ] Geburtstag 5/A3
bite [baɪt] beißen 6/B1
black [blæk] schwarz 1/B3
blow out [bləʊ‿'aʊt] ausblasen 5/C2
blue [bluː] blau 1/A5
board [bɔːd] Tafel 1/C2
boat [bəʊt] Boot 1/B5
body ['bɒdi] Körper 2/A2
book [bʊk] Buch 1/A8
boot [buːt] Stiefel 3/A8
bored [bɔːd] gelangweilt 5/A3
boring ['bɔːrɪŋ] langweilig 4/C7
bottle ['bɒtl] Flasche 2/C2
bottom ['bɒtəm] Grund 1/O; Hinterteil 2/A4
box [bɒks] Schachtel 3/C2
boy [bɔɪ] Junge 1/A8
bread [bred] Brot 2/C2
break [breɪk] Pause 5/A5
breakfast ['brekfəst] Frühstück 2/A2
bridge [brɪdʒ] Brücke 6/B2
bring [brɪŋ] (mit)bringen 3/A2
° British ['brɪtɪʃ] britisch 1/O
° brochure ['brəʊʃə] Broschüre 5/O
brother ['brʌðə] Bruder 4/A5
brown [braʊn] braun 1/B3
brush [brʌʃ] (ab)bürsten 5/A9
bull [bʊl] Stier, Bulle 6/B71
bullfighter ['bʊlˌfaɪtə] Stierkämpfer/in 6/C3
bull-riding ['bʊlˌraɪdɪn] Bullenreiten 6/C4
busy ['bɪzi] beschäftigt 4/B1
but [bət] aber 2/A2
° butter ['bʌtə] Butter 2/B6
buy [baɪ] kaufen 1/B1
buyer ['baɪə] Käufer/in 5/B8
bye *(informal)* [baɪ] tschüs 2/C6

C

cage [keɪdʒ] Käfig 3/C4
cake [keɪk] Kuchen 1/A5
° cake pan ['keɪk ˌpæn] Kuchenform 2/B6
calendar ['kæləndə] Kalender 5/B2
call [kɔːl] nennen 4/B5
it's called [ɪts 'kɔːld] es heißt 3/B6
° calm down [kɑːm 'daʊn] sich beruhigen 6/O
camera ['kæm(ə)rə] Kamera, Fotoapparat 5/C1
can [kən] können 1/I
candle ['kændl] Kerze 5/C2
canteen [kæn'tiːn] Kantine 4/C8
cap [kæp] Mütze, Kappe 5/B5
car [kɑː] Auto 4/C6

card [kɑːd] Karte 1/A7
careful ['keəfl] vorsichtig 3/C2
carpet ['kɑːpɪt] Teppich 4/B1
carrot ['kærət] Karotte 5/B5
carry ['kæri] tragen 5/C1
cat [kæt] Katze 1/A8
'cause (= because) [kəz, bɪ'kɒz] weil, da 4/A5
CD [ˌsiː'diː] CD W
CD player [siː'diː ˌpleɪə] CD-Player 4/A3
cereal *(no pl)* ['sɪəriəl] Frühstückszerealien *(Cornflakes, Müsli …)* 2/B2
chain [tʃeɪn] Kette 4/C9
chair [tʃeə] Stuhl 4/A3
change [tʃeɪndʒ] Wechselgeld 5/B5
change [tʃeɪndʒ] (ver)ändern; wechseln 3/A7; tauschen 4/C4
chant [tʃɑːnt] Sprechchor 3/A9
charity ['tʃærəti] wohltätiger Zweck 6/C4
chat [tʃæt] Unterhaltung, Plauderei 4/A3
°chat [tʃæt] plaudern; sich unterhalten; chatten 6/O
°check [tʃek] überprüfen, kontrollieren 5/O
cheese [tʃiːz] Käse 2/C2
chestnut ['tʃesˌnʌt] Kastanie 4/B4
chicken ['tʃɪkɪn] Huhn 2/C2
child (*pl* **children**) [tʃaɪld, 'tʃɪldrən] Kind 3/A6
°chin [tʃɪn] Kinn 3/O3
°Chinese [ˌtʃaɪ'niːz] Chinese/Chinesin; chinesisch 1/O
chips *(npl)* [tʃɪps] Pommes 2/C2
chocolate *(no pl)* ['tʃɒklət] Schokolade 4/B5
choose [tʃuːz] auswählen 3/A9
Christmas ['krɪsməs] Weihnachten 5/B5
cinema ['sɪnəmə] Kino 4/B4
°cinnamon ['sɪnəmən] Zimt 2/B6
circle ['sɜːkl] Kreis 1/C6
°clap [klæp] klatschen 1/O
class [klɑːs] (Schul)klasse 1/B6
class [klɑːs] Unterricht 5/A3
classmate ['klɑːsˌmeɪt] Klassenkamerad/in 1/A7
classroom ['klɑːsˌruːm] Klassenzimmer 1/A7
clean [kliːn] sauber machen; putzen 4/B1
°clean [kliːn] sauber 3/O1
clear [klɪə] klar; aufgeräumt 4/A5
°clock [klɒk] Uhr 2/O2
close [kləʊs] schließen, zumachen 1/C4
clothes *(npl)* [kləʊðz] Kleider, Kleidung 1/B5
cloudy ['klaʊdi] bewölkt, bedeckt 6/B5
club [klʌb] Klub 1/A8
coach [kəʊtʃ] Trainer 3/A8
cock [kɒk] Hahn 6/B6
coffee ['kɒfi] Kaffee 2/B2
coke [kəʊk] Cola W
cold [kəʊld] Erkältung 3/A5
cold [kəʊld] kalt 4/B4
be cold [bi 'kəʊld] frieren 4/B4
collage ['kɒlɑːʒ] Collage 1/C3
collect [kə'lekt] sammeln 3/A4
colour ['kʌlə] Farbe 1/C8
°colouring pencil [ˌkʌlərɪŋ 'pensl] Buntstift 5/O
comb [kəʊm] Kamm 2/A5
come [kʌm] kommen 3/A2
Come on! [kʌm‿'ɒn] Komm jetzt!, Mach schon! 2/A2
compare [kəm'peə] vergleichen 5/A7
competition [ˌkɒmpə'tɪʃn] Wettbewerb 6/A2
°conker ['kɒŋkə] Rosskastanie 1/O
contest ['kɒntest] Wettbewerb 6/C4
contact ['kɒntækt] Kontakt 3/A2
°cook [kʊk] Koch/Köchin 6/O
cook [kʊk] kochen 4/B1
correct [kə'rekt] richtig, korrekt 5/C2
count [kaʊnt] zählen 1/B7
country ['kʌntri] Land 3/A2
of course [əv 'kɔːs] natürlich 3/A2
court [kɔːt] Court, Platz 3/B2
cousin ['kʌzn] Cousin/e 2/A8
°cover ['kʌvə] bedecken 2/B6
cow [kaʊ] Kuh 6/A2
cowgirl ['kaʊˌgɜːl] Cowgirl 6/C3
°crazy ['kreɪzi] verrückt 2/O1
crocodile ['krɒkəˌdaɪl] Krokodil 3/C1
°cross [krɒs] durchqueren; überqueren 1/O
cry [kraɪ] weinen 5/C1
CU (= See you.) ['siː jə] Bis bald. 1/A8
cucumber ['kjuːˌkʌmbə] (Salat)gurke 5/B5
cup [kʌp] Tasse; *hier:* Pokal; Cup 3/A2
cupboard ['kʌbəd] Schrank 2/B2
curly ['kɜːli] Ringel- 6/B6
°curtain ['kɜːtən] Vorhang 6/O
cut [kʌt] schneiden 5/C1
°C ya. (= See you.) ['siː jə] Bis bald. 6/O

D

dachshund ['dæksnd] Dackel 3/C7
dairy ['deəri] Milchprodukte 2/C2
dance [dɑːns] Tanz 5/C2
dance [dɑːns] tanzen 4/C6
dancing ['dɑːnsɪŋ] Tanzen W
dancing class ['dɑːnsɪŋ ˌklɑːs] Tanzunterricht 4/C8
°in the dark [ˌɪn ðə 'dɑːk] im Dunkeln 3/O2
dark [dɑːk] dunkel 2/A6
date [deɪt] Datum 5/B1
daughter ['dɔːtə] Tochter 5/C4
day [deɪ] Tag 3/A3
°dead [ded] tot 6/O
dear [dɪə] Schatz, Engel 4/B5
dear … [dɪə] liebe/r … 4/A5
Oh dear. [əʊ 'dɪə] Du meine Güte! 3/A5
December [dɪ'sembə] Dezember 5/C1
decorate ['dekəˌreɪt] schmücken 5/C1
decoration [ˌdekə'reɪʃn] Dekoration 5/C1
°deep [diːp] tief 1/O
deep-sea [ˌdiːp'siː] Tiefsee- 6/A2
describe [dɪ'skraɪb] beschreiben 2/A6
delicious [de'lɪʃəs] köstlich, lecker 4/B1
design and technology [dɪˌzaɪn‿ənd tek'nɒlədʒi] *erweiterter Werkunterricht* 5/A5
desk [desk] Schreibtisch 4/A3
°detective [dɪ'tektɪv] Kriminalbeamte/r; (Privat)detektiv/in 6/O
detective story [dɪ'tektɪv ˌstɔːri] Kriminalroman; Detektivgeschichte 6/A2
dictionary ['dɪkʃənri] Wörterbuch 4/C8

difficult ['dɪfɪklt] schwierig, schwer 5/A5
dining-room ['daɪnɪŋ ˌruːm] Esszimmer 2/B2
dirt *(no pl)* [dɜːt] Schmutz 2/A5
dirty ['dɜːti] dreckig, schmutzig 2/A5
divorced [dɪ'vɔːst] geschieden 5/C4
do [duː] machen, tun 3/B5
do the shopping [ˌduː ðə 'ʃɒpɪŋ] einkaufen (gehen) 4/B1
do the washing up [ˌduː ðə ˌwɒʃɪŋ‿'ʌp] abspülen 4/B1
Do you have ...? [ˌduː jʊ 'hæv] Hast du/Haben Sie ...? 1/C1
dog [dɒg] Hund 1/A8
door [dɔː] Tür 1/C2
°Dr (= Doctor) ['dɒktə] Dr. 6/O
drama ['drɑːmə] Theater 6/A2
draw [drɔː] zeichnen 2/A6
°drawer ['drɔːə] Schublade 4/O
dream [driːm] Traum 3/C7
dream [driːm] träumen 5/A3
dress [dres] sich anziehen 5/A9
drink [drɪŋk] Getränk 2/B1
drink [drɪŋk] trinken 4/C7
drop [drɒp] fallen lassen 4/B4
°drums *(pl)* [drʌmz] Schlagzeug 6/O
duck [dʌk] Ente 6/B6
°dust *(no pl)* [dʌst] Staub 4/O
DVD [ˌdiːviː'diː] DVD 5/B5

E

each [iːtʃ] jede(r, s) 5/A9
each other [ˌiːtʃ‿'ʌðə] einander 6/C2
ear [ɪə] Ohr 2/A2
easy ['iːzi] einfach 4/C1
eat [iːt] essen 2/B4
egg [eg] Ei 2/B2
elbow ['elbəʊ] Ellbogen 2/A4
elephant ['elɪfənt] Elefant 4/A4
Anything else? [ˌeniθɪŋ‿'els] Darf es noch etwas sein? 2/C6
emoticon [ɪ'məʊtɪˌkɒn] Emoticon 6/O
end [end] Ende, Schluss 5/B3
in the end [ˌɪn ðiː‿'end] letzten Endes 6/C3
England ['ɪŋglənd] England 1/A7
English ['ɪŋglɪʃ] englisch 1/C2
in English [ɪn‿'ɪŋglɪʃ] auf Englisch 3/B4
°enter ['entə] Auftritt 6/O
European [jʊərə'piːən] europäische(r, s) 3/A2
every ['evri] jede(r, s) 5/A6
everyone ['evriwʌn] jede(r); alle W
everywhere ['evriweə] überall 6/B1
example [ɪg'zɑːmpl] Beispiel 5/C3
excited [ɪk'saɪtɪd] aufgeregt, gespannt 3/A5
exciting [ɪk'saɪtɪŋ] aufregend; spannend 6/C3
Excuse me! [ɪks'kjuːz ˌmi] Entschuldigen Sie bitte!, Entschuldigung 5/B5
exercise book ['eksəsaɪz ˌbʊk] Heft 1/C2
exhibition [ˌeksɪ'bɪʃn] Ausstellung 6/C4
exit ['eksɪt] Ausgang 4/B4
expert ['ekspɜːt] Experte/Expertin 6/C4
explain [ɪk'spleɪn] erklären 6/C4
eye [aɪ] Auge 2/A2

F

face [feɪs] Gesicht 2/A4
fact [fækt] Tatsache 6/C4
fall [fɔːl] fallen 6/C2
family ['fæmli] Familie 3/A2
family name ['fæmli ˌneɪm] Nachname, Familienname 4/B5
family tree ['fæmli ˌtriː] Familienstammbaum 5/C4
fantastic *(informal)* [fæn'tæstɪk] fantastisch 6/B5
fantasy ['fæntəsi] Fantasie 5/C6
farm [fɑːm] Bauernhof 6/A2
farmer ['fɑːmə] Bauer/Bäuerin, Farmer/in 6/C3
fascinating ['fæsɪneɪtɪŋ] faszinierend 6/C4
fast [fɑːst] schnell 3/A5
father ['fɑːðə] Vater 5/B3
favourite ['feɪv(ə)rət] Lieblings- 1/A7
February ['februəri] Februar 5/C1
feed [fiːd] zu essen geben, füttern 4/C1
feel [fiːl] (sich) fühlen 5/A3
felt-tip [ˌfelt'tɪp] Filzstift 1/C2
°female ['fiːmeɪl] weiblich 6/O
fill in [fɪl‿'ɪn] ausfüllen; einfügen 6/B6
final ['faɪnl] Endspiel 3/A2
find [faɪnd] finden 1/A1
find out [faɪnd‿'aʊt] herausfinden 4/A5
fine [faɪn] in Ordnung, gut 4/A3
finger ['fɪŋger] Finger 2/A4
finish ['fɪnɪʃ] beenden, aufhören 1/A8
first [fɜːst] zuerst; als Erstes 4/B1
first name ['fɜːst ˌneɪm] Vorname 4/B5
fish [fɪʃ] Fisch 3/C1
°fish finger [ˌfɪʃ 'fɪŋgə] Fischstäbchen 2/O2
flat [flæt] Wohnung 3/C2
floor [flɔː] Boden 4/A5
°flour ['flaʊə] Mehl 2/B6
fly [flaɪ] fliegen 3/C9
foggy ['fɒgi] neblig 6/B5
folder ['fəʊldə] Mappe, Schnellhefter 1/C2
follow ['fɒləʊ] folgen 2/C2
food *(no pl)* [fuːd] Essen, Nahrung 2/B1
food technology [ˌfuːd tek'nɒlədʒi] Ernährungslehre 4/C7
foot (*pl* **feet**) [fʊt, fiːt] Fuß 2/A2
football *(no pl)* ['fʊtbɔːl] Fußball 1/I
for [fɔː] für 3/A4
for now [fə 'naʊ] fürs Erste 6/B6
for sale [fə 'seɪl] zu verkaufen 3/A2
forget [fə'get] vergessen 4/A3
free [friː] frei, gratis 2/C4
free time [ˌfriː 'taɪm] Freizeit 3/I
°freeze [friːz] gefrieren; einfrieren 1/O
freezer ['friːzə] Gefrierschrank 2/C2
French [frentʃ] Franzose/Französin; französisch; Französisch 5/A5
°fresh [freʃ] frisch 3/O1
friend [frend] Freund/in 1/I
make friends [meɪk 'frendz] sich anfreunden 1/A8
friendly match [ˌfrendli 'mætʃ] Freundschaftsspiel 3/A2
from [frəm] von, aus 1/I
in front of [ɪn 'frʌnt‿əv] vor 2/A2
frozen ['frəʊzn] (tief)gefroren 2/C2

fruit [fruːt] Obst 5/B5
fun *(no pl)* [fʌn] Spaß 5/A3
funny ['fʌni] lustig, witzig, komisch 3/A2
furry ['fɜːri] pelzig 2/A5

G

game [geɪm] Spiel 1/I
°garden ['gɑːdn] Garten 3/O2
gear [gɪə] Ausrüstung, Sachen 4/A6
geography [dʒiː'ɒgrəfi] Erdkunde, Geografie 5/A5
German ['dʒɜːmən] deutsch 1/C1
in German [ɪn 'dʒɜːmən] auf Deutsch 3/B4
Germany ['dʒɜːməni] Deutschland 1/A6
get [get] erhalten, bekommen 2/C4; werden 6/B4
get off [get‿'ɒf] aussteigen (aus) 4/B3
get on [get‿'ɒn] einsteigen (in) 4/B3
get through [get 'θruː] durchgehen, durchkommen 5/B5
get up [get‿'ʌp] aufstehen 5/A9
girl [gɜːl] Mädchen 1/I
give [gɪv] geben 3/A2
glass [glɑːs] Glas 5/C1
glasses *(npl)* ['glɑːsɪz] Brille 1/B7
go [gəʊ] gehen 2/A2; werden 5/A3
go on [gəʊ‿'ɒn] weitermachen 1/C6; weitergehen 6/B2
go out [gəʊ‿'aʊt] ausgehen 4/C7
goal [gəʊl] Tor 3/B3
goalkeeper ['gəʊlˌkiːpə] Tormann/Torfrau 3/A8
goat [gəʊt] Ziege 6/B1
°golden ['gəʊld(ə)n] aus Gold, golden, Gold- 1/O
goldfish *(pl* **goldfish***)* ['gəʊldˌfɪʃ] Goldfisch 1/A8
good [gʊd] gut 2/I
good-looking [ˌgʊd'lʊkɪŋ] gut aussehend 2/A6
goose *(pl* **geese***)* [guːs, giːs] Gans 6/B3
grammar ['græmə] Grammatik 5/C3
granddaughter ['grænˌdɔːtə] Enkelin 5/C4
grandfather ['grænˌfɑːðə] Großvater 5/C4
grandma ['grænˌmɑː] Oma, Omi 5/C1
grandmother ['grænˌmʌðə] Großmutter 5/C4
grandson ['grænˌsʌn] Enkel 5/C4
grass *(pl* -es) [grɑːs, grɑːsɪz] Gras 6/B3
graze [greɪz] grasen, weiden 6/B3
great [greɪt] großartig, wunderbar 1/A8
Greek [griːk] Grieche/Griechin; griechisch W
green [griːn] grün 1/B3
grey [greɪ] grau 1/B3
grid [grɪd] Tabelle 4/C4
group [gruːp] Gruppe 4/A5
guest [gest] Gast 5/C2
guitar [gɪ'tɑː] Gitarre 6/A3
guy [gaɪ] Kerl, Typ 2/A6
gym (= gymnasium) [dʒɪm, dʒɪm'neɪziəm] Turnhalle 3/A2

H

had [hæd] (→ have) hatte/hatten 3/B4
hair *(no pl)* [heə] Haar(e) 2/A2
hairbrush ['heəˌbrʌʃ] Haarbürste 2/A5
half [hɑːf] halb 2/A5
half past (three) [ˌhɑːf pɑːst ('θriː)] halb (vier) (Uhr) 6/B1
hamster ['hæmstə] Hamster W
hand [hænd] Hand 2/A2
°hand of the clock [hænd‿əv ðə klɒk] Uhrzeiger 2/O2
handball ['hændˌbɔːl] Handball 3/B2
hang [hæŋ] (auf)hängen 1/A7
happen ['hæpən] geschehen, passieren 5/C2
happy ['hæpi] glücklich; zufrieden; fröhlich 3/C3
Happy birthday [ˌhæpi 'bɜːθdeɪ] Alles Gute zum Geburtstag 5/B1
hard [hɑːd] kräftig 1/O; hart 4/C3
hat [hæt] Hut 1/B5
hate [heɪt] hassen 2/A6
have [həv] haben 1/A8; essen; trinken 2/B1
I'll have [aɪl 'hæv] ich hätte gern 6/B4
°have got [həv 'gɒt] haben 6/O
°have lunch [həv 'lʌntʃ] zu Mittag essen 6/O
°hazel ['heɪzl] haselnussbraun 6/O
head [hed] Kopf 2/A4
hear [hɪə] hören 4/B4
hedgehog ['hedʒˌhɒg] Igel 3/C1
hello [hə'ləʊ] hallo 1/I
help [help] Hilfe 3/B2
help [help] helfen 4/A5
helper ['helpə] Helfer/in; Gehilfe 4/C3
here [hɪə] hier 4/A6
Here you are. [ˌhɪə juː‿'ɑː] Hier, bitte!, Bitte schön! 1/C1
history ['hɪst(ə)ri] Geschichte 5/A5
°hit [hɪt] (zu)schlagen 1/O
holidays *(npl)* ['hɒlɪdeɪz] Ferien, Urlaub 1/B5
home [həʊm] Zuhause 3/A2
at home [æt 'həʊm] zu Hause 3/B6
home town [ˌhəʊm 'taʊn] Heimatstadt 6/B5
homework *(no pl)* ['həʊmˌwɜːk] Hausaufgaben 4/A3
hoover ['huːvə] staubsaugen 4/B1
horse [hɔːs] Pferd 3/B6
hot [hɒt] heiß 4/B4
house [haʊs] Haus 3/C4
how [haʊ] wie 4/B3
How are you? [haʊ‿'ɑː ˌjʊ] Wie geht es dir/Ihnen/euch? 4/B5
how much [ˌhaʊ 'mʌtʃ] wie viel 2/C5
How much is/are ...? [ˌhaʊ mʌtʃ‿'ɪz/'ɑː] Was kostet/kosten ...? 2/C5
°hug [hʌg] Umarmung 6/O
hungry ['hʌŋgri] hungrig 6/B1
be in a hurry [ˌbi‿ɪn‿ə 'hʌri] es eilig haben, in Eile sein 5/C1
hurry up [ˌhʌri‿'ʌp] sich beeilen 2/A2
husband ['hʌzbənd] Ehemann 5/C4

I

I [aɪ] ich 1/I
I can't wait. [aɪ ˌkɑːnt 'weɪt] Ich kann's kaum erwarten. 3/A5
I'll have [aɪl 'hæv] ich hätte gern 6/B4
I'm sorry. [aɪm 'sɒri] Das tut mir Leid. 3/A5

I've made new friends already [aɪv ˌmeɪd njuː ˌfrendz͜ɔːl'redi] Ich habe schon neue Freunde gefunden 1/A8
ice cream [ˌaɪs 'kriːm] Eiskrem, Eis 6/B4
idea [aɪ'dɪə] Idee 4/A3
° if [ɪf] wenn, falls 1/O
in [ɪn] in 1/A2
° in turns [ɪn 'tɜːnz] abwechselnd 1/O
information *(no pl)* [ˌɪnfə'meɪʃn] Information 3/A2
information and communication technology [ɪnfəˌmeɪʃn͜ənd kəmjuːnɪˌkeɪʃn tek'nɒlədʒi] Informatik 5/A5
inline skating *(no pl)* [ˌɪnlaɪn 'skeɪtɪŋ] Inline-Skaten W
inside [ɪn'saɪd] innen; im Inneren 5/A9
interest ['ɪntrəst] Interesse 6/A3
interested ['ɪntrəstɪd] interessiert 5/A3
be interested in [bi͜'ɪntrəstɪd͜ɪn] sich interessieren für 6/A1
interesting ['ɪntrəstɪŋ] interessant 5/A5
interview ['ɪntəˌvjuː] befragen 6/A2
into ['ɪntʊ] in 3/C3
introduce [ˌɪntrə'djuːs] vorstellen 4/B5
invitation [ˌɪnvɪ'teɪʃn] Einladung 5/A3
invite [ɪn'vaɪt] einladen 4/A3
it [ɪt] es 1/B2
It's [ɪts] er/sie/es kostet 2/C5
It's me. [ɪts 'miː] Ich bin's. 3/B1
Italian [ɪ'tæliən] Italiener(in); italienisch 3/B5

J

jam [dʒæm] Marmelade 2/B2
January ['dʒænjuəri] Januar 5/C4
job [dʒɒb] Arbeit, Tätigkeit 4/B1
join [dʒɔɪn] mitmachen bei; beitreten 3/A2
joke [dʒəʊk] Witz 3/B5
° joking ['dʒəʊkɪŋ] scherzhaft; scherzend 6/O
judo ['dʒuːdəʊ] Judo 3/B6
July [dʒʊ'laɪ] Juli 6/C4
° jump [dʒʌmp] springen 1/O
June [dʒuːn] Juni 5/B2
just [dʒʌst] einfach 4/B5; nur 5/B5
Just a minute [ˌdʒʌst͜ə 'mɪnɪt] Einen Augenblick/Moment 4/A3

K

karate [kə'rɑːti] Karate 3/B6
keep [kiːp] (be)halten, aufbewahren 3/C2
kick [kɪk] treten, schießen, kicken 3/A9
kick out [kɪk͜'aʊt] hinauswerfen, hinausschmeißen 3/B4
° kill [kɪl] töten 6/O
° kiss [kɪs] Kuss 6/O
kit [kɪt] Trikot 3/A8
kitchen ['kɪtʃən] Küche 2/B5
kitten ['kɪtn] Kätzchen, junge Katze 3/A2
knee [niː] Knie 2/A4
knife (*pl* **knives**) [naɪf, naɪvz] Messer 6/A2
know [nəʊ] wissen, kennen 5/I

L

label ['leɪbl] beschriften 1/C3
lady ['leɪdi] Frau, Dame 2/C2
lamb [læm] Lamm 6/B1
° lamp [læmp] Lampe 4/O
last [lɑːst] letzte(r, s) 5/A3
late [leɪt] (zu) spät 1/C1
lazy ['leɪzi] faul 4/C1
learn [lɜːn] lernen 3/A9
least [liːst] am wenigsten 3/C9
leave [liːv] verlassen 5/A3
left [left] (nach) links 6/B2
leg [leg] Bein 2/A4
lemonade [ˌlemə'neɪd] Limonade 6/B4
lesson ['lesn] Stunde 5/A3
° let [let] lassen 6/O
Let's ... [lets] Lass(t) uns ... 4/C1
Let's go. [lets 'gəʊ] Los! 1/I
letter ['letə] Buchstabe 5/C5
° library ['laɪbrəri] Bibliothek, Bücherei 6/O
life (*pl* **lives**) [laɪv, laɪvz] Leben 4/C1
like [laɪk] mögen 1/A8
like [laɪk] wie 6/A2
like this [laɪk 'ðɪs] so 1/A6
list [lɪst] Liste 4/B2
listen to ['lɪsn] zuhören 1/A2
a little [ə 'lɪtl] ein bisschen 3/B5
live [lɪv] leben, wohnen W
living room ['lɪvɪŋ ˌruːm] Wohnzimmer 4/B1
° loaf of bread [ˌləʊf͜əv 'bred] Brotlaib 1/O
long [lɒŋ] lang 2/A6
° look [lʊk] sehen; aussehen 4/O
look at [lʊk͜æt] betrachten, sehen 1/A1
look for ['lʊk fə] suchen nach 3/A2
look up [lʊk͜'ʌp] nachschlagen 6/C4
loser ['luːzə] Verlierer/in 3/B3
a lot (of) [ə 'lɒt (əv)] viel(e); sehr 1/A8
a lot [ə 'lɒt] sehr 3/A8
° lots of ['lɒts͜əv] viel, jede Menge 4/O
love [lʌv] lieben, sehr gern mögen 5/A3
lovely ['lʌvli] schön, hübsch 5/B5
lucky number [ˌlʌki 'nʌmbə] Glückszahl 1/B9
lunch [lʌntʃ] Mittagessen 4/B1

M

magazine [ˌmægə'ziːn] Zeitschrift, Magazin 2/C2
main hall [meɪn 'hɔːl] Haupthalle 6/C4
make [meɪk] machen 1/A6
make friends [meɪk 'frendz] sich anfreunden 1/A8
° make sure [ˌmeɪk 'ʃɔː] sich versichern, darauf achten 3/O1
° male [meɪl] männlich 6/O
man (*pl* men) [mæn, men] Mann 2/A7
many ['meni] viele 4/B3
map [mæp] (Land)karte 1/B4
March [mɑːtʃ] März 5/B2
market ['mɑːkɪt] Markt 1/B1
marmalade *(no pl)* ['mɑːməˌleɪd] *Marmelade aus Zitrusfrüchten* 2/B2
married ['mærɪd] verheiratet 5/C4
match [mætʃ] zuordnen 3/A4
maths *(informal)* [mɑːθs] Mathe 4/C6
May [meɪ] Mai 5/C1
mean [miːn] bedeuten; meinen 4/B3
meet [miːt] (sich) treffen 4/B4
melon ['melən] Melone 1/B7
member ['membə] Mitglied 3/A2

middle ['mɪdl] Mitte 3/A7
milk [mɪlk] Milch 2/B2
milk [mɪlk] melken 6/A2
not mind [nɒt 'maɪnd] nichts dagegen haben 2/C2
mindmap ['maɪndmæp] Wortnetz 3/B4
mineral water ['mɪn(ə)rəl ˌwɔːtə] Mineralwasser 6/B4
minute ['mɪnɪt] Minute 1/C4
mirror ['mɪrə] Spiegel 2/A2
°mixture ['mɪkstʃə] Mischung 2/B6
money *(no pl)* ['mʌni] Geld 6/C4
month [mʌnθ] Monat 5/B1
moon [muːn] Mond 6/C4
more [mɔː] mehr 3/A2
morning ['mɔːnɪŋ] Morgen 2/A1
mother ['mʌðə] Mutter 2/A2
Mother's day ['mʌðəz ˌdeɪ] Muttertag 4/C1
°mouse (*pl* mice) [maʊs, maɪs] Maus 3/O3
°moussaka *(no pl)* [muː'sɑːkə] Moussaka 4/B1
mouth [maʊθ] Mund 2/A4
move [muːv] Bewegung 6/A2
°move on [muːv‿'ɒn] sich wieder auf den Weg machen; weitergehen 1/O
Mr ['mɪstə] Herr *(Anrede)* 3/A2
Mrs ['mɪsɪz] Frau *(Anrede)* 3/A2
°much [mʌtʃ] viel; sehr 3/O3
murderer ['mɜːdərə] Mörder/in 6/C1
museum [mjuː'ziːəm] Museum 6/A2
mushroom ['mʌʃruːm] Pilz 2/B2
music ['mjuːzɪk] Musik 1/A8
must [mʌst] müssen 4/A3

N

name [neɪm] Name 1/A4
near [nɪə] nahe 3/B6
neat [niːt] ordentlich, sauber 2/A5
neck [nek] Nacken 2/A4
need [niːd] brauchen 3/A5
neighbour ['neɪbə] Nachbar/in 4/B4
nephew ['nefjuː] Neffe 5/C4
never ['nevə] nie(mals) 4/C1
new [njuː] neu 3/A2
news *(no pl)* [njuːz] Nachrichten 3/B3
newspaper ['njuːzˌpeɪpə] Zeitung 6/A2
next [nekst] nächste(r, s) 3/A2
next [nekst] dann, gleich darauf; als Nächstes 5/C2
next to ['nekst‿tə] neben 2/C2
°nibble ['nɪbl] knabbern 3/O3
nice [naɪs] schön, nett 1/A8
niece [niːs] Nichte 5/C4
night [naɪt] Nacht 4/A3
°at night [ət 'naɪt] nachts 3/O1
no [nəʊ] nein 1/A5; kein(e) 6/B4
°no one ['nəʊ ˌwʌn] niemand 3/O3
no. (= number) ['nʌmbə] Nr. 4/C6
noisy ['nɔɪzi] laut 5/B5
normally ['nɔːm(ə)li] normalerweise 4/C1
nose [nəʊs] Nase 2/A2
not [nɒt] nicht 1/A5
notice ['nəʊtɪs] Anzeige; Notiz 3/A4
notice ['nəʊtɪs] bemerken 5/C3
noticeboard ['nəʊtɪsˌbɔːd] Aushang, schwarzes Brett 3/A2
November [nəʊ'vembə] November 5/C1
now [naʊ] jetzt 3/A5
for now [fə 'naʊ] fürs Erste 6/B6
number ['nʌmbə] Zahl; Ziffer; Nummer 4/B4

O

(three) o'clock [(θriː) ə'klɒk] (drei) Uhr 1/C6
October [ɒk'təʊbə] Oktober 1/O
of [əv] von 1/A7
of course [əv 'kɔːs] natürlich 3/A2
special offer [ˌspeʃl‿'ɒfə] Sonderangebot 2/C2
often ['ɒfn] oft 4/C1
Oh dear. [əʊ 'dɪə] Du meine Güte! 3/A5
old [əʊld] alt 2/A7
on [ɒn] auf 2/B2; am, an 3/A2
onion ['ʌnjən] Zwiebel 2/C2
only ['əʊnli] nur 4/C1; einzige(r, s) 6/O
°onto ['ɒntə] auf 6/O
open ['əʊpən] öffnen 4/B4
open ['əʊpən] offen, geöffnet 2/A5
open day ['əʊpən ˌdeɪ] Tag der offenen Tür 6/C1
or [ɔː] oder 2/A4
orange ['ɒrɪndʒ] Orange 5/B5
orange ['ɒrɪndʒ] orange(farben) 1/B3
orange juice *(no pl)* ['ɒrɪndʒ ˌdʒuːs] Orangensaft 2/C2
order ['ɔːdə] Ordnung, Reihenfolge 5/C2
organize ['ɔːgəˌnaɪz] ordnen, sortieren 3/B4
other ['ʌðə] andere(r, s) 1/B2
out [aʊt] draußen 6/B1
out and about [ˌaʊt‿ənd‿ə'baʊt] unterwegs 6/I
°out of ['aʊt‿əv] aus 3/O1
outing ['aʊtɪŋ] Ausflug 6/A2
outside [ˌaʊt'saɪd] im Freien, draußen 6/B1
°oven ['ʌvn] (Back)ofen, Backrohr 2/B6
over ['əʊvə] über 6/B2
be over [bi‿'əʊvə] vorbei/aus sein 5/A9
over there [ˌəʊvə 'ðeə] dort drüben 1/I
own [əʊn] eigene(r, s) 6/A2

P

page [peɪdʒ] Blatt; Seite 1/B1
palace ['pæləs] Palast 4/B4
°paper ['peɪpə] Papier 5/O
parents ['peərənts] Eltern 4/B4
park [pɑːk] Park W
part [pɑːt] Teil 2/A2
take part (in) [ˌteɪk 'pɑːt] teilnehmen (an) 6/A2
past [pɑːst] nach 5/A9
pen [pen] Stift 1/C1
°pen pal ['pen ˌpæl] Brieffreund/in 6/O
pencil ['pensl] Bleistift 1/C1
pencil case ['pensl ˌkeɪs] Federmäppchen 1/C2
penny (*pl* pence) [peni, pens] Penny 2/C4
people *(pl)* ['piːpl] Leute 4/B4
perfect ['pɜːfɪkt] vollkommen, perfekt 2/A6
performance [pə'fɔːməns] Vorführung 6/C4
perhaps [pə'hæps] vielleicht 5/A3
person ['pɜːsn] Person, Mensch 5/C2
pet [pet] Haustier 3/C1
phone [fəʊn] Telefon 1/C8
phone [fəʊn] anrufen 3/A5
photo ['fəʊtəʊ] Foto 5/C1

phrase [freɪz] Satz; Ausdruck, (Rede)wendung 5/B8
physical education *(no pl)* [ˌfɪzɪkl‿edjʊ'keɪʃn] Sport(unterricht) 5/A5
pick up [pɪk‿'ʌp] aufheben 4/B4
picture ['pɪktʃə] Bild 3/A4
pig [pɪg] Schwein 6/B1
piglet ['pɪglət] Ferkel 6/B2
place [pleɪs] Ort; Platz 3/A3
plan [plæn] Plan W
° plan [plæn] planen 5/O
planet ['plænɪt] Planet 6/A2
planetarium *(pl -s or -ria)* [ˌplænə'teəriəm, ˌplænə'teəriəmz, ˌplænə'teəriə] Planetarium 6/A2
plant [plɑːnt] Pflanze 4/B1
play [pleɪ] Spiel; (Theater)stück 6/A2
play [pleɪ] spielen 1/I
play a trick on sb [ˌpleɪ‿ə 'trɪk‿ɒn ˌsʌmbədi] jdm einen Streich spielen 4/C1
player ['pleɪə] Spieler/in 3/A5
playing field ['pleɪɪŋ ˌfiːld] Sportplatz 3/B2
please [pliːz] bitte 1/C1
poem ['pəʊɪm] Gedicht 2/A8
point [pɔɪnt] Stelle, Punkt 6/B2
point (to) [pɔɪnt] deuten/zeigen (auf) 2/A2
° police *(npl)* [pə'liːs] Polizei 6/O
Polish ['pɒlɪʃ] polnisch 3/B5
pony ['pəʊni] Pony 3/C8
° poodle ['puːdl] Pudel 1/O
poor [pɔː] arm 4/B4
postcard ['pəʊstˌkɑːd] Postkarte 6/B5
poster ['pəʊstə] Poster 1/C2
potato *(pl* **-es)** [pə'teɪtəʊ, pə'teɪtəʊz] Kartoffel 5/B5
pound [paʊnd] Pfund 2/C4
practise ['præktɪs] üben 6/A2
° preheat (to) [priː'hiːt (tə)] vorheizen (auf) 2/B6
preparation [ˌprepə'reɪʃn] Vorbereitung 5/C1
prepare [prɪ'peə] vorbereiten 5/C1
present ['preznt] Geschenk 5/B4
present (to) [prɪ'zent] bieten; präsentieren 2/A8
president ['prezɪdənt] Präsident/in 1/A8
press-up ['presʌp] Liegestütz 3/B5
price [praɪs] Preis 5/B8
prince [prɪns] Prinz 1/A7
problem ['prɒbləm] Problem 3/A5
project ['prɒdʒekt] Projekt 3/A2
pullover ['pʊləʊvə] Pullover 2/C5
pupil ['pjuːpl] Schüler/in 5/A3
purple ['pɜːpl] violett 1/B3
put [pʊt] setzen, stellen, legen 3/C2
put on ['pʊt‿ɒn] anziehen 3/A9
puzzle out [ˌpʌzl‿'aʊt] herausfinden, herausbekommen 1/A3

Q

question ['kwestʃn] Frage 3/A4
quick [kwɪk] schnell 3/C2
quite [kwaɪt] ziemlich 4/A5

R

rabbit ['ræbɪt] Kaninchen 1/A10
° raccoon [rə'kuːn] Waschbär/in 3/O2
rain [reɪn] Regen 6/B5
rain [reɪn] regnen 6/B4
rainy ['reɪni] regnerisch 6/B5
° rather ['rɑːðə] ziemlich 3/O3
° reach [riːtʃ] erreichen 1/O
read [riːd] lesen 1/A4
ready ['redi] fertig 4/A5
° real [rɪəl] wirklich 6/O
really ['rɪəli] wirklich W
record [rɪ'kɔːd] aufnehmen 1/C8
red [red] rot 1/A8
registration [ˌredʒɪ'streɪʃn] Anmeldung 5/A5
religious education [rəˌlɪdʒəs‿edjʊ'keɪʃn] Religionslehre 5/A5
repair [rɪ'peə] reparieren 4/C6
° reply [rɪ'plaɪ] antworten 1/O
report [rɪ'pɔːt] Bericht 6/A2
reporter [rɪ'pɔːtə] Reporter/in 6/A2
° restaurant ['rest(ə)rɒnt] Restaurant 1/O
° rhyme *(no pl)* [raɪm] Reim 1/O
° rhyming ['raɪmɪŋ] Reim- 3/O3
ride (on) [raɪd] Fahrt (mit) 6/C3
ride [raɪd] fahren 3/B5; reiten 3/C8
right [raɪt] richtig 1/B6
right [raɪt] gut, ok 2/C2
be right [bi 'raɪt] Recht haben 4/C1
ring [rɪŋ] klingeln, läuten 5/A3
rinse [rɪns] spülen 2/A5
° river ['rɪvə] Fluss 1/O
road [rəʊd] Straße 3/C2
role [rəʊl] Rolle 1/A5
roll [rəʊl] Brötchen 2/C6
room [ruːm] Zimmer, Raum 4/A1
rubber ['rʌbə] Radiergummi 1/C2
rubbish *(no pl)* ['rʌbɪʃ] Müll 4/C1
rucksack ['rʌkˌsæk] Rucksack 6/B1
° rule [ruːl] Regel 1/O
ruler ['ruːlə] Lineal 1/C1
run [rʌn] laufen, rennen 3/A5
° run about [ˌrʌn‿ə'baʊt] herumrennen 3/O3
Russian ['rʌʃn] Russe/Russin; russisch 3/B5

S

° sad [sæd] traurig 6/O
safe [seɪf] sicher 5/A9
° sailor ['seɪlə] Matrose, Seemann 1/O
for sale [fə 'seɪl] zu verkaufen 3/A2
the same [ðə 'seɪm] der-/die-/dasselbe 2/A3
° sanctuary ['sæŋktʃuəri] Tierpflegestation 3/O2
sausage ['sɒsɪdʒ] Wurst, Würstchen 2/B2
say [seɪ] sagen 1/A9
scarf *(pl -s or* scarves) [skɑːf, skɑːvz] Schal 3/A2
school [skuːl] Schule 1/B4
schoolbag ['skuːlbæg] Schultasche 1/C1
science *(no pl)* ['saɪəns] (Natur)wissenschaft 5/A5
scone [skəʊn] *brötchenartiges Gebäck* 6/B4
score [skɔː] Punktestand; Spielstand 3/B3
score [skɔː] schießen 3/B3
scored [skɔːd] (→ score) schoss/schossen 3/B3
sea *(no pl)* [siː] Meer 2/A2
° go to sea [ˌgəʊ tə 'siː] zur See gehen 1/O
see [siː] sehen 1/A1
See you on ... ['siː jə‿ˌɒn] Bis ... 3/A5

°seem [siːm] scheinen 3/O3
sell [sel] verkaufen 5/B5
seller ['selə] Verkäufer/in 5/B8
sentence ['sentəns] Satz 6/C4
September [sep'tembə] September 5/C5
set the table [ˌset ðə 'teɪbl] den Tisch decken 4/B1
shampoo *(no pl)* [ʃæm'puː] Shampoo 2/A5
shark *(pl -s or -)* [ʃɑːk, ʃɑːks] Hai(fisch) 6/C1
she [ʃɪ] sie 1/I
sheep *(pl* **sheep**) [ʃiːp] Schaf 6/B1
shelf *(pl* **shelves**) [ʃelf, ʃelvz] Regal 4/A3
shine [ʃaɪn] scheinen; glänzen, leuchten 5/A9
shirt [ʃɜːt] Shirt, Hemd 3/A2
°shocked [ʃɒkt] schockiert, entsetzt 6/O
shoe [ʃuː] Schuh 3/A7
shop [ʃɒp] Geschäft, Laden 1/B2
shop assistant ['ʃɒp‿əˌsɪstnt] Verkäufer/in 2/C2
shopping *(no pl)* ['ʃɒpɪŋ] Einkaufen 2/A2
do the shopping [ˌduː ðə 'ʃɒpɪŋ] einkaufen (gehen) 4/B1
shopping list ['ʃɒpɪŋ ˌlɪst] Einkaufsliste 2/A2
short [ʃɔːt] kurz 2/A6
should [ʃʊd] sollen 2/A5
shoulder ['ʃəʊldə] Schulter 2/A4
show [ʃəʊ] zeigen 6/A2
°side [saɪd] Seite 1/O
sightseeing *(no pl)* ['saɪtˌsiːɪŋ] Besichtigungen, Sightseeing 6/A2
sign [saɪn] (Straßen-/Verkehrs)schild 6/B1
sing along [ˌsɪŋ‿ə'lɒŋ] mitsingen 1/A1
singer ['sɪŋə] Sänger/in 3/A2
single parent [ˌsɪŋgl 'peərənt] Alleinerziehende/r 5/C4
Sir [sɜː] Herr *(Anrede)* 5/A3
sister ['sɪstə] Schwester 2/B5
sit [sɪt] sitzen 1/C6
°sit down [sɪt 'daʊn] sich (hin)setzen 6/O
size [saɪz] Größe 3/A2
skating *(no pl)* ['skeɪtɪŋ] Rollerskaten 6/A2
°skipping *(no pl)* ['skɪpɪŋ] Seilspringen 1/O
sleep [sliːp] schlafen 4/A3
sleepover ['sliːpˌəʊvə] Übernachtung 4/A3
slim [slɪm] schlank, schmal, dünn 2/A6
small [smɔːl] klein 3/C2
smell [smel] Geruch; Duft; Gestank 6/B1
smile [smaɪl] lächeln 5/A3
snack bar ['snæk ˌbɑː] Imbissstube 6/B1
snail [sneɪl] Schnecke 3/C2
snow [snəʊ] Schnee 4/B4
snowball ['snəʊˌbɔːl] Schneeball 4/B4
snowy ['snəʊi] schneereich 6/B5
so [səʊ] so 1/A8; also 2/C2
soap [səʊp] Seife 2/A5
sock [sɒk] Socke 5/B5
°sofa ['səʊfə] Sofa, Couch 4/O
°soft [sɒft] weich 3/O1
sold out [səʊld‿'aʊt] ausverkauft 5/B5
some [sʌm] einige; etwas 4/B4
someone ['sʌmwʌn] jemand 2/A8
something ['sʌmθɪŋ] etwas 5/B8
sometimes ['sʌmtaɪmz] manchmal 4/C1
son [sʌn] Sohn 5/C4
sorry ['sɒri] Verzeihung, Entschuldigung; wie bitte? 1/C1
I'm sorry. [aɪm 'sɒri] Das tut mir Leid. 3/A5
°sort of ['sɔːt‿əv] so 'ne Art von 6/O
sound [saʊnd] klingen, sich anhören 6/A2
space *(no pl)* [speɪs] Weltraum 6/A2
speak [spiːk] sprechen 3/B5
special edition [ˌspeʃl‿ɪ'dɪʃn] Sonderausgabe 6/C4
special offer [ˌspeʃl‿'ɒfə] Sonderangebot 2/C2
spider ['spaɪdə] Spinne 3/C1
sport [spɔːt] Sport(art) 1/A8
°sports [spɔːts] Sport 4/A6
sports centre ['spɔːts‿ˌsentə] Sportcenter 3/B2
°spring [sprɪŋ] Frühling 4/O
°spring-cleaning *(no pl)* [ˌsprɪŋ 'kliːnɪŋ] Frühjahrsputz 4/O
stable ['steɪbl] Stall, Box 3/C8
stage [steɪdʒ] Bühne 6/A2
stall [stɔːl] (Verkaufs)stand 5/B5
stamp [stæmp] Briefmarke 6/B1
stand [stænd] stehen 3/B5
star [stɑː] Stern 6/A2
start [stɑːt] Anfang, Beginn 2/I
start [stɑːt] anfangen 5/A5
station ['steɪʃn] Bahnhof 4/A3
stay [steɪ] bleiben 4/A3
stay up late [ˌsteɪ‿ʌp 'leɪt] lang aufbleiben 4/C7
°step [step] Schritt 1/O
stick [stɪk] kleben 1/C8
still [stɪl] (immer) noch 2/A6
°stool [stuːl] Hocker 4/O
stop [stɒp] aufhören, beenden 5/C1
stormy ['stɔːmi] stürmisch 6/B5
story ['stɔːri] Geschichte, Erzählung 4/C4
straight [streɪt] gerade(aus) 2/A5; glatt 2/A7
strawberry ['strɔːb(ə)ri] Erdbeere 6/B4
street [striːt] Straße 1/B2
streetball ['striːtˌbɔːl] Streetball; Basketball auf dem Freiplatz 3/B2
strong [strɒŋ] stark 2/A6
subject ['sʌbdʒɪkt] (Schul)fach 5/A5
sugar ['ʃʊgə] Zucker 2/B2
sun [sʌn] Sonne 6/C4
sunglasses *(npl)* ['sʌnˌglɑːsɪz] Sonnenbrille 1/B2
sunny ['sʌni] sonnig 6/B5
°superduper *(informal)* [ˌsuːpə'duːpə] ganz toll, absolut super 2/B6
supermarket ['suːpəˌmɑːkɪt] Supermarkt 2/C1
support [sə'pɔːt] unterstützen 3/A9
sure [ʃɔː] sicher 2/C2
°make sure [ˌmeɪk 'ʃɔː] sich versichern, darauf achten 3/O1
survey ['sɜːveɪ] Untersuchung, Umfrage 1/B9
°sweep [swiːp] kehren 4/O
swim [swɪm] schwimmen 3/C9

T

table ['teɪbl] Tisch 2/A2
table tennis ['teɪbl ˌtenɪs] Tischtennis 3/A2
tail [teɪl] Schwanz 6/B6
take [teɪk] (mit)nehmen 3/C2
take a photo [ˌteɪk‿ə 'fəʊtəʊ] ein Foto machen 5/C1

take out [teɪk‿'aʊt] hinausbringen 4/C1
take part (in) [ˌteɪk 'pɑːt] teilnehmen (an) 6/A2
talk [tɔːk] Gespräch; Unterhaltung 6/C2
talk (to) [tɔːk] sprechen/reden (mit) 1/A3
tall [tɔːl] groß 2/A6
tea [tiː] Tee 2/B5
teacher ['tiːtʃə] Lehrer/in 5/A3
telescope ['telɪˌskəʊp] Teleskop 6/A3
tell [tel] erzählen 3/B5
tell [tel] sagen 1/A8
terrarium (*pl* -s *or* -ria) [tə'reəriəm] Terrarium 3/O1
terrible ['terəbl] schrecklich, furchtbar 6/B5
thank you ['θæŋk ˌjə] danke 2/C2
thanks [θæŋks] danke 1/A5
that [ðæt] der/die/das (da drüben) 2/A2
that's [ðæts] das kostet 2/C6
That's me. [ðæts 'miː] Das bin ich. 2/A6
the [ðə] der/die/das 1/I
theatre ['θɪətə] Theater 6/C1
their [ðeə] ihr(e) 1/A8
them [ðem] sie, ihnen 2/A3
theme (1) [θiːm ('wʌn)] Kapitel (1) 1/I
then [ðen] dann 3/A5
there is/are [ðeər‿'ɪz/'ɑː] es gibt, da sind 1/B2
these (*pl of* this) [ðiːz] diese 4/A6
they [ðeɪ] sie 1/A3
they are [ðeɪ‿'ɑː] sie kosten 2/C5
thing [θɪŋ] Ding, Gegenstand 2/C5
think [θɪŋk] (nach)denken, glauben, meinen 3/C6
this [ðɪs] diese(r, s); das 1/I
like this [laɪk 'ðɪs] so 1/A6
this is ['ðɪs‿ɪz] das ist/sind 1/A7
those (*pl of* **that**) [ðəʊz] diese; jene 5/B5
through [θruː] durch 2/C2
°throw out [θrəʊ‿'aʊt] hinauswerfen 4/O
thumb [θʌm] Daumen 2/A4
tick [tɪk] Haken 4/C6
tick [tɪk] abhaken 4/C6
tidy ['taɪdi] ordentlich 4/A5
tidy up [ˌtaɪdi‿'ʌp] aufräumen 4/A3
tiger ['taɪgə] Tiger 3/C1
till [tɪl] bis 5/A9
time [taɪm] (Uhr)zeit 3/A3
time [taɪm] Mal 4/B4
What time is it? [ˌwɒt‿taɪm‿'ɪz‿ɪt] Wie viel Uhr ist es? 1/C1
timetable ['taɪmteɪbl] Stundenplan 5/A5
°tip [tɪp] Rat(schlag), Tipp 3/O1
tired ['taɪəd] müde 4/C3
to [tə] in, nach, zu, an 1/A8
today [tə'deɪ] heute 5/A3
toe [təʊ] Zeh(e) 2/A4
together [tə'geðə] zusammen, gemeinsam 1/A8
toilet ['tɔɪlət] Toilette, Klo 6/B1
toilet bag ['tɔɪlət ˌbæg] Kulturbeutel, Toilettentasche 2/A5
tomato (*pl* **-es**) [tə'mɑːtəʊ, tə'mɑːtəʊz] Tomate 5/B5
tomorrow [tə'mɒrəʊ] morgen 3/A5
tongue twister ['tʌŋ ˌtwɪstə] Zungenbrecher 5/B3
too [tuː] auch 1/A8
tooth (*pl* **teeth**) [tuːθ, tiːθ] Zahn 2/A2
toothbrush ['tuːθˌbrʌʃ] Zahnbürste 2/A5
toothpaste ['tuːθˌpeɪst] Zahnpasta 2/A5
on top of [ɒn 'tɒp‿əv] auf 2/A5
°touch [tʌtʃ] berühren 3/O3
track [træk] Anlage 6/C4
tractor ['træktə] Traktor 6/A2
°traffic ['træfɪk] Verkehr 2/O2
°traffic jam ['træfɪk ˌdʒæm] Stau 2/O2
train [treɪn] Zug 4/B4
training ['treɪnɪŋ] Training 3/A8
tree [triː] Baum 6/B2
trick [trɪk] Trick, List; Kunststück 1/B7
trip [trɪp] Ausflug 6/A2
trolley ['trɒli] Einkaufswagen 2/C4
°true [truː] wahr 3/O2
°try [traɪ] versuchen, probieren 6/O
try out [traɪ‿'aʊt] ausprobieren, testen 5/C1
the tube [ðə 'tjuːb] die (Londoner) U-Bahn 4/B3
tummy ['tʌmi] Bauch 2/A4
Turkish ['tɜːkɪʃ] türkisch 3/B5
turn [tɜːn] abbiegen 6/B2
°in turns [ɪn 'tɜːnz] abwechselnd 1/O
TV (= television) [ˌtiː'viː, 'telɪˌvɪʃn] Fernseher, Fernsehen 4/B1
twin [twɪn] Zwilling, Zwillings- W

U

ugh *(informal)* [ʌg] i!, igitt! W
ugly ['ʌgli] hässlich 2/A6
uncle ['ʌŋkl] Onkel 5/C1
under ['ʌndə] unter 4/A3
underline [ˌʌndə'laɪn] unterstreichen 6/C3
underwater [ˌʌndə'wɔːtə] Unterwasser- 6/C4
unhappy [ʌn'hæpi] unglücklich 5/A3
unicycle ['juːnɪˌsaɪkl] Einrad 3/B5
uniform ['juːnɪˌfɔːm] Uniform 4/A4
untidy [ʌn'taɪdi] unordentlich 4/A5
up [ʌp] nach oben 1/B7
use [juːz] benutzen 5/C2

V

vanilla *(no pl)* [və'nɪlə] Vanille 6/B4
vegetable ['vedʒtəbl] Gemüse 5/B5
verse [vɜːs] Strophe 5/A9
very ['veri] sehr 3/A2
very much [ˌveri 'mʌtʃ] sehr 6/C3
°vet [vet] Tierarzt, Tierärztin 3/O1
video ['vɪdiəʊ] Video 5/B5
visit ['vɪzɪt] Besuch 4/A3
visit ['vɪzɪt] besuchen 6/A2
°volunteer [ˌvɒlən'tɪə] Freiwillige/r 4/O

W

°wake up [ˌweɪk‿'ʌp] aufwecken 3/O1
walk [wɔːk] Spaziergang 4/B4
walk [wɔːk] (zu Fuß) gehen 3/C9
walk on [wɔk‿'ɒn] weitergehen 5/B5
walk past [wɔːk 'pɑːst] vorbeigehen 5/B5
wall [wɔːl] Wand 4/A6

°wanna (= want to) ['wɒnə] willst du 6/O
want [wɒnt] wünschen; wollen 3/A2
wardrobe ['wɔːdrəʊb] Kleiderschrank 4/A3
warm [wɔːm] warm 4/B4
was [wɒz] (→ be) war 3/B3
wash [wɒʃ] waschen 2/A5
do the washing up [ˌduː ðə ˌwɒʃɪŋ‿'ʌp] abspülen 4/B1
watch [wɒtʃ] zusehen, zuschauen; ansehen 6/A2
watch out [wɒtʃ‿'aʊt] aufpassen, sich in Acht nehmen 4/A5
watch out for [ˌwɒtʃ‿'aʊt fə] Ausschau halten nach 1/B7
watch TV [ˌwɒtʃ tiː'viː] fernsehen 4/B1
water *(no pl)* ['wɔːtə] Wasser 2/A2
water ['wɔːtə] gießen 4/B1
way [weɪ] Weg 2/C2; Art und Weise 4/I
we [wiː] wir 1/I
wear [weə] tragen 3/A8
weather ['weðə] Wetter 6/B5
week [wiːk] Woche 4/C7
weekend [ˌwiːk'end] Wochenende 5/B5
welcome ['welkəm] willkommen W
well [wel] nun (ja), tja 1/A8
were [wɜː] (→ be) warst/waren/wart 3/B3
wet [wet] nass 6/B4
what [wɒt] was 1/I
°wheel [wiːl] Rad 3/O1
when [wen] wann; wenn 3/A2
where [weə] wo 3/A2
which [wɪtʃ] welche(r, s) 2/A6
°whisker ['wɪskə] Schnurrhaar 1/O
whistle ['wɪsl] pfeifen 3/B5
white [waɪt] weiß 1/B3
who [huː] wer, wem, wen 1/I
whose [huːz] wessen 5/C5
why [waɪ] warum 3/A5
wife (*pl* wives) [waɪf, waɪvz] Ehefrau 5/C4
wiggle ['wɪgl] wackeln mit 3/B5
wild [waɪld] wild 3/C2
win [wɪn] gewinnen 3/B3
window ['wɪndəʊ] Fenster 4/A3
windy ['wɪndi] windig 6/B5
winner ['wɪnə] Gewinner/in; Sieger/in 3/B3
winter ['wɪntə] Winter 4/B4
all winter [ˌɔːl 'wɪntə] den ganzen Winter 6/B1
°wipe [waɪp] abwischen, abputzen 4/O
with [wɪð] mit W
woman (*pl* **women**) ['wʊmən, 'wɪmɪn] Frau 2/A7
won [wʌn] (→ win) gewann/gewannen 3/B3
°wonderful ['wʌndəfl] wunderbar, wundervoll 6/O
word [wɜːd] Wort 2/A1
work *(no pl)* [wɜːk] Arbeit 2/A2
work [wɜːk] funktionieren 1/B7
Work with a partner. [ˌwɜːk wɪθ‿ə 'pɑːtnə] Arbeite mit einem/einer Partnerin zusammen. 1/A1
worksheet ['wɜːkˌʃiːt] Arbeitsblatt 4/C5
°world [wɜːld] Welt 6/O
worry ['wʌri] sich Sorgen machen 6/B1
would [wʊd] würde 3/C8
write [raɪt] schreiben 1/A7
write down [raɪt 'daʊn] aufschreiben 2/A6
wrong [rɒŋ] falsch 1/B6

Y

°yard [jɑːd] (Hinter)hof 1/O
year [jɪə] Schuljahr 3/A2; Jahr 5/C4
yellow ['jeləʊ] gelb 1/B3
yes [jes] ja 1/I
yesterday ['jestədeɪ] gestern 6/B5
°yoghurt ['jɒgət] Joghurt 2/B6
you [jʊ] du, dich, dir; Sie, Ihnen; ihr, euch 1/I
young [jʌŋ] jung 3/A2
yours [jɔːz] deine(r, s), Ihre(r, s) 6/B5
yourself (*pl* yourselves) [jə'self, jə'selvz] dich, dir 2/A6
youth club ['juːθ ˌklʌb] Jugendzentrum 4/B4
yuck *(informal)* [jʌk] i, igitt 4/C1
yummy *(informal)* ['jʌmi] lecker 1/B7
yup *(informal)* [jʌp] ja 2/B2

Z

zoo [zuː] Zoo 6/B5

A

abbiegen turn
aber but
abspülen do the washing up
alle(s) all
alt old
am on
an at, on, to
Änderung change
Anfang beginning
anfangen start
anrufen phone
ansehen watch
Antwort answer
antworten answer
Anzeige notice
Apfel apple
April April
Arbeit job
Arbeite mit einem/einer Partner/in zusammen. Work with a partner.
Arm arm
auch too
auf at, on
aufbewahren keep
aufhören stop
aufräumen tidy up
aufregend exciting
Auge eye
August August
aus from
Ausflug outing, trip
auswählen choose
Auto car

B

Bad(ezimmer) bathroom
Bahnhof station
Banane banana
Bauer/Bäuerin farmer
Bauernhof farm
Baum tree
beantworten answer
beenden stop
behalten keep
bei at
Bein leg
bekommen get
bemerken notice
benutzen use
beschreiben describe
betrachten look at
Bett bed
bewölkt cloudy
bieten present (to)
Bild picture
ich bin I'm (= I am)
Ich bin's. It's me.
bitte please
Wie bitte? Sorry
bitten ask
Blatt *(Papier)* page
blau blue
Bleistift pencil
Boden floor
brauchen need
braun brown
Briefmarke stamp
bringen bring
Brot bread
Brücke bridge
Bruder brother
Buch book
Bulle bull

C

CD-Player CD player

D

da ist/sind there is/are
danke thank you, thanks
dann then
das the, this
das (da drüben) that
das kostet that's
Das tut mir Leid. I'm sorry.
den Tisch decken set the table
dein(e) your
(nach)denken think
der the
der (da drüben) that
deuten (auf) point (to)
deutsch German
auf Deutsch in German
Deutschland Germany
Dezember December
dich you
die the
die (da drüben) that
Dienstag Tuesday
diese these, those
diese(r, s) this
Ding thing
dir you
Donnerstag Thursday
draußen outside
dritte(r, s) third
du you

E

Ei egg
ein(e) a/an
ein(e, er, es) one
einfach easy
einige some
Einkaufen shopping *(no pl)*
einkaufen (gehen) do the shopping
noch einmal again
Eiskrem, Eis ice cream
Elefant elephant
Eltern parents
England England
englisch English
auf Englisch in English
Ente duck
Entschuldigen Sie bitte! Excuse me!
Entschuldigung Sorry, Excuse me!
er he
erste(r, s) first
erzählen tell
Erzählung story
es it
Es freut mich, dich/Sie kennen zu lernen. Nice to meet you.
es gibt there is/are
Es kostet It's
Essen food *(no pl)*
essen eat, have
etwas some
euch you

F

Fach subject
fahren ride
Fahrrad bike
falsch wrong
Familie family
Familienname family name
fantastisch fantastic *(informal)*
Farbe colour
Farmer/in farmer
faul lazy
Februar February
Federmäppchen pencil case
Fenster window
Ferkel piglet
fernsehen watch TV
fertig ready
finden find
Finger finger
fliegen fly
Foto photo
Fotoapparat camera
Frage question
fragen ask
Frau woman (*pl* women), Mrs *(Anrede)*
im Freien outside
Freitag Friday

Freund/in friend
ein Foto machen take a photo
fröhlich happy
Frühstück breakfast
fühlen feel
für for
Fuß foot (*pl* feet)
Fußball football *(no pl)*
füttern feed

G

Gans goose (*pl* geese)
Gast guest
geben give
Geburtstag birthday
Alles Gute zum Geburtstag Happy birthday
Gefrierschrank freezer
gegen against
gehen go, walk
Wie geht es dir/Ihnen/euch? How are you?
Worum geht es in/bei ...? What is ... about?
gelangweilt bored
gelb yellow
Geld money *(no pl)*
Gemüse vegetable
sehr gern mögen love
Geschäft shop
Geschenk present
Geschichte story
Gesicht face
gestern yesterday
Getränk drink
gewinnen win
es gibt there is/are
gießen water
Gitarre guitar
Glas glass
glücklich happy
Goldfisch goldfish
grau grey
groß big, tall
großartig great
Großmutter grandmother
Großvater grandfather
grün green
Gruppe group
Gurke cucumber
gut good

H

Haar(e) hair *(no pl)*
haben have
Hahn cock
halb (vier) (Uhr) half past (three)
hallo hello
halten keep
Hand hand
Haus house
Hausaufgaben homework *(no pl)*
zu Hause at home
Haustier pet
Heft exercise book
heiß hot
ich heiße I'm (= I am), my name is
Wie heißt du?, Wie heißen Sie? What's your name?
helfen help
herausfinden find out
Herr *(Anrede)* Mr, Sir
heute today
hier here
Hier, bitte! Here you are.
Hilfe help
hinausbringen take out
hinter behind
hören hear
hübsch lovely
Huhn chicken
Hund dog
hungrig hungry

I

ich I
ich bin I'm (= I am)
Ich bin's. It's me.
ich heiße I'm (= I am), my name is
Idee idea
Igel hedgehog
ihm him
ihn him
ihnen them
Ihnen you
Wie geht es Ihnen? How are you?
ihr you
ihr(e) their, its
ihr(e, n) her
im Freien outside
immer always
in at, in, to
interessant interesting
sich interessieren für be interested in
interessiert interested

J

ja yes
Jahr year
Januar January
jede(r, s) every
jene those
jetzt now
Juli July
Juni June
Junge boy

K

Kaffee coffee
Käfig cage
kalt cold
Kamera camera
Kaninchen rabbit
Karotte carrot
Kartoffel potato (*pl* -es)
Käse cheese
Katze cat
kaufen buy
kennen know
Es freut mich, dich/Sie kennen zu lernen. Nice to meet you.
Kerze candle
Kind child (*pl* children)
Klasse class
Klassenkamerad/in classmate
Klassenzimmer classroom
Kleider, Kleidung clothes *(npl)*
Kleiderschrank wardrobe
klein small
kochen cook
kommen come
Wo kommst du her? Where are you from?
können can
Kopf head
Korb basket
Körper body
köstlich delicious
korrekt correct
sie kosten they are
er/sie/es kostet it's
das kostet ... that's ...
Was kostet/kosten ...? How much is/are ...?
Küche kitchen
Kuh cow
kurz short

L

Laden shop
Lamm lamb
lang long
langweilig boring
laufen run
laut noisy
Leben life (*pl* lives)
lecker delicious

legen put
Lehrer/in teacher
Das tut mir Leid. I'm sorry.
lernen learn
lesen read
letzte(r, s) last
Leute people *(pl)*
lieben love
Lieblings- favourite
Limonade lemonade
Lineal ruler
links left
Liste list
lustig funny

M

machen do, make, take
Mädchen girl
März March
Mai May
manchmal sometimes
Mann man (*pl* men)
Markt market
mehr more
mein(e) my
Messer knife (*pl* knives)
mich me
Milch milk
Mineralwasser mineral water
mir me
mitbringen bring
mitnehmen take
Mittagessen lunch
Mittwoch Wednesday
mögen like
Mond moon
Montag Monday
Morgen morning
morgen tomorrow
müde tired
Müll rubbish *(no pl)*
Mund mouth
Musik music
müssen must
Mutter mother
Mütze cap

N

nach to, after
nach links left
Nachbar/in neighbour
Nachmittag afternoon
Nachname family name
nachschlagen look up
nächste(r, s) next
nahe near
Nahrung food
Name name
Nase nose
nass wet
natürlich of course
neben next to
neblig foggy
nehmen take
nein no
nett nice
neu new
nicht not
nie(mals) never
noch einmal again
normalerweise normally
November November
Nummer number

O

Obst fruit
oder or
oft often
Ohr ear
Oktober October
Onkel uncle
Orange orange
Orangensaft orange juice *(no pl)*
Ordnung order
Ort place

P

Pause break
Penny penny (*pl* pence)
Pferd horse
Pflanze plant
Pfund pound
Platz place
Pommes chips *(npl)*
Postkarte postcard
präsentieren present (to)
Preis price
putzen clean

R

Rad bike
Radiergummi rubber
Raum room
reden (mit) talk (to)
Regal shelf (*pl* shelves)
Regen rain
regnen rain
regnerisch rainy
Reihenfolge order
reiten ride
rennen run
Reporter/in reporter
richtig correct, right
rot red

S

sagen say
sammeln collect
Samstag Saturday
Satz sentence
sauber machen clean
Schachtel box
Schaf sheep (*pl* sheep)
Scheune barn
schlafen sleep
Schnee snow
schneereich snowy
schneiden cut
schnell fast
schön nice, beautiful, lovely
Schrank cupboard
schreiben write
Schreibtisch desk
Schuh shoe
Schule school
Schüler/in pupil
Schulfach subject
Schulklasse class
Schultasche schoolbag
schwarz black
Schwein pig
schwer difficult
Schwester sister
schwierig difficult
schwimmen swim
sehen see, look at
sehr very, a lot (of)
sehr gern mögen love
sein be
sein(e) its
sein(e, r) his
Seite page
September September
setzen put
sicher sure
sie she, they, them
Sie kosten They are
Sie you
Da sind There is/are
Socke sock
Sohn son
Sonnabend Saturday
Sonne sun
sonnig sunny
Sonntag Sunday
spannend exciting
Spaß fun *(no pl)*
spielen play
Spiele die Szene nach. Act the scene.
Sport sport
sprechen speak
sprechen (mit) talk (to)

Stand stall
stark strong
staubsaugen hoover
stellen put
Stern star
Stier bull
Stift pen
Straße street, road
Stuhl chair
Stunde lesson
Stundenplan timetable
stürmisch stormy
suchen nach look for
Supermarkt supermarket

T

Tafel board
Tag day
Tante aunt
Tanz dance
tanzen dance
Tätigkeit job
Tee tea
Teil part
Teppich carpet
Tier animal
Tisch table
den Tisch decken set the table
Tochter daughter
Toilette toilet
Tomate tomato (*pl* -es)
Traum dream
(sich) treffen meet
trinken drink, have
tschüs bye *(informal)*
tun do
Das tut mir Leid. I'm sorry.

U

üben practise
über about
halb (vier) Uhr half past (three)
Wie viel Uhr ist es? What time is it?
Uhrzeit time
und and
unglücklich unhappy
unordentlich untidy
uns us
unser(e) our
unter under

V

Vater father
verärgert angry
vergessen forget
vergleichen compare
verkaufen sell
Verkäufer/in shop assistant
Verkaufsstand stall
verlassen leave
Verzeihung sorry
viel(e) a lot (of)
viele many
Vogel bird
von from
vor in front of
vorbereiten prepare
Vorname first name

W

Wand wall
wann when
warm warm
warum why
was what
Was ist mit …? What about …? *(informal)*
Was kostet/kosten …? How much is/are …?
Wasser water *(no pl)*
Wechselgeld change
Weihnachten Christmas
weinen cry
weiß white
wem who
wen who
wenn when
wer who
wessen whose
Wetter weather
wie how, like
Wie bitte? Sorry
Wie geht es dir/Ihnen/euch? How are you?
Wie heißt du?, Wie heißen Sie? What's your name?
Wie viel Uhr ist es? What time is it?
Wie wäre es mit …? What about …? *(informal)*
wieder again
windig windy
Winter winter
wir we
wissen know
witzig funny
wo where
Wo kommst du her? Where are you from?
Woche week
Wochenende weekend
Wohnzimmer living room
wollen want
Wort word
Wörterbuch dictionary
Wortnetz mindmap
Worum geht es in/bei …? What is … about?
wunderbar great
wünschen want
wütend angry
Wurst, Würstchen sausage

Z

Zahl number
Zahn tooth (*pl* teeth)
zeichnen draw
zeigen (auf) point (to)
Zeit time
Zeitung newspaper
Ziege goat
Ziffer number
Zimmer room
zornig angry
zu to
zu essen geben feed
zu Hause at home
Zucker sugar
zufrieden happy
zuhören listen to
zuordnen match
zuschauen, zusehen watch
zweite(r, s) second
Zwiebel onion

Girls/Women

Alice ['ælɪs]
Amy ['eɪmi]
Brenda ['brendə]
Caroline ['kær(ə)laɪn]
Claire [kleə]
Emma ['emə]
Erica ['erɪkə]
Ethel ['eθl]
Fay [feɪ]
Gill [dʒɪl]
Gillian ['dʒɪlɪən]
Gwen [gwen]
Jane [dʒeɪn]
Janet ['dʒænɪt]
Jelouna [dʒə'luːnə]
Jessica ['dʒesɪkə]
Jill [dʒɪl]
Josephine ['dʒəʊzəˌfiːn]
Lilian ['lɪliən]
Lilli ['lɪli]
Lynn [lɪn]
Mandy ['mændi]
Mary ['meəri]
Maybel ['meɪbl]
Michelle [mɪ'ʃel]
Nina ['niːnə]
Selina [sə'liːnə]
Sharon ['ʃærən]

Boys/Men

Alexej [æ'lekseɪ]
Bernie ['bɜːni]
Bob [bɒb]
Brad [bræd]
Charlie ['tʃɑːli]
David ['deɪvɪd]
George [dʒɔːdʒ]
Harry ['hæri]
Ivor ['aɪvə]
Jack [dʒæk]
Kenny ['keni]
Mark [mɑːk]
Morgan ['mɔːgən]
Murat ['mʊræt]
Nikos ['nɪkɒs]
Nino ['niːnəʊ]
Pete [piːt]
Philipp ['fɪlɪp]
Rajiv [rɑː'dʒiːv]
Robert ['rɒbət]
Ron [rɒn]
Steven ['stiːvn]
Tadeusz ['tædjuːs]
Tony ['təʊni]
Will [wɪl]
Zoltan ['zɒltən]

Families

Baker ['beɪkə]
Batson ['bætsn]
Baxter ['bækstə]
Blake [bleɪk]
Coggins ['kɒgɪnz]
Collins ['kɒlɪnz]
Dean [diːn]
Dixon ['dɪksn]
Goldman ['gəʊldmən]
Graham ['greɪəm]
Green [griːn]
Khan [kɑːn]
Mason ['meɪsn]
McDonald [mək'dɒnəld]
Perrakis [pə'rɑːkɪs]
Ram [ræm]
Roberts ['rɒbəts]
Scott [skɒt]
Simmons ['sɪmənz]
Smith [smɪθ]
Tan Fong [ˌtæn 'fɒŋ]
Thorn [θɔːn]
West [west]
Williams ['wiljəmz]

Other Names

Abba ['æbə]
Arsenal Chelsea [ˌɑːsnl 'tʃelsi]
Big Ben [ˌbɪg 'ben]
Buckingham Palace [ˌbʌkɪŋəm 'pæləs]
Eurodisney ['jʊərəʊˌdɪzni]
Fuzzy ['fʌzi]
Hendon School [ˌhendən 'skuːl]
Henrietta [ˌhenri'etə]
Holland Park School [ˌhɒlənd pɑːk 'skuːl]
Hoover ['huːvə]
Kentish Town City Farm [ˌkentɪʃ taʊn 'sɪti fɑːm]
Max [mæks]
MC [ˌem'siː]
Mme Tussaud's [ˌmædəm tʊ'sɔːdz]
Radio Junior Europe [ˌreɪdiəʊ ˌdʒuːniə 'jʊərəp]
Rocket ['rɒkɪt]
Sammy ['sæmi]
Sandy ['sændi]
Shetland ['ʃetlənd]
Socks [sɒks]
St Paul's [sənt 'pɔːlz]
Tarzan ['tɑːzn]
Westminster Abbey [ˌwestmɪnstər‿'æbi]

Geographical Names

Australia [ɒ'streɪliə]
Budapest [ˌbjuːdə'pest]
Camden ['kæmdən]
Cologne [kə'ləʊn]
Europe ['jʊərəp]
Finland ['fɪnlənd]
France [frɑːns]
Germany ['dʒɜːməni]
Hendon ['hendən]
Hendon Central [ˌhendən 'sentrəl]
Holland Park [ˌhɒlənd 'pɑːk]
Hungary ['hʌŋgəri]
Istanbul ['ɪstænˌbʊl]
Italy ['ɪtəli]
Kings Cross St. Pancras [ˌkɪŋz krɒs‿sən 'pæŋkrəs]
London ['lʌndən]
Manchester ['mæntʃɪstə]
Moscow ['mɒskəʊ]
New York [ˌnjuː'jɔːk]
Notting Hill [ˌnɒtɪŋ 'hɪl]
Paris ['pærɪs]
Pisa ['piːzə]
Poland ['pəʊlənd]
Portobello Road [pɔːtəʊˌbeləʊ 'rəʊd]
Russia ['rʌʃə]
Sweden ['swiːdn]
Sydney ['sɪdni]
Turkey ['tɜːki]
Ulvila [ʌl'viːlə]
United States [juːˌnaɪtɪd 'steɪts]
USA (= United States of America) [ˌjuːes'eɪ, jʊːˌnaɪtɪd ˌsteɪts‿əv‿əmerɪkə]
Warsaw ['wɔːsɔː]
West Avenue [ˌwest 'ævənjuː]
Westbourne Park Station [ˌwestbɔːn pɑːk 'steɪʃn]

Quellenverzeichnis

Bildquellen

Umschlag außen: blum DESIGN & KOMMUNIKATION, Hamburg
Innenumschlag vorn: Dr. Peter Güttler, Berlin (Karte London)

11 Christine Huwer, Frankfurt a.M. (Portobello Road Market); Kerstin Klemm, Braunschweig (Hendon School); Jessica Hatcher, Frankfurt a.M. (Schild, Laden)

15 Kraus, Silvestris, Kastl (Paris); Roland Witschel, dpa, Hamburg (Pisa); Silvestris/PhotoPress, s.e.t. Photoproductions, Kastl (New York); Schoefman, Silvestris/PhotoPress, Kastl (Köln); Peter, Gundelfingen (Istanbul); Rose, Silvestris/PhotoPress, Kastl (Dresden); Kuzmiuk, Silvestris/PhotoPress, Kastl (Warschau); Michael Rieke, Hannover (Sydney); Christian Krug, Münster (Moskau)

16 Corbis, Düsseldorf (Prinz Harry), Interfoto, München (Abba); Renate Krause, Ettlingen (Mädchen); Michael Blöß, Linz (Jungs)

19 Jens Bolhöfer, Hannover (Schild); Christine Huwer, Frankfurt (Marktstände); Ruth Barker, Plauen (Kinder am Computer)

21 Ruth Barker, Plauen (Umfrage)

22/23 Getty Images, London (Covent Garden)

25 Ruth Barker, Plauen (Kinder in der Klasse)

26 Alex Sturrock/Network Photographers/Agentur Focus, Hamburg (Bobby); Kirstin Jebautzke, Braunschweig (15 Uhr); age fotostock/Mauritius, Hamburg (6:33, 7:26); Corbis, Düsseldorf (7:14); age fotostock/Mauritius, Hamburg (16 Uhr)

27 Ruth Barker, Plauen (Junge)

28 Martin Parr/Magnum Photos/Agentur Focus, Hamburg (Mädchen beim Spielen); Nicole Bergemann, Braunschweig (conkers)

29 Valérie Callaghan, Braunschweig (Supermarkt, Tafel, Sonderangebot); Barry Lewis/Network Photographers/Agentur Focus, Hamburg (Frühstück)

33 Tanja Ripke, Hamburg (Kinder)

35 J. Walmsley, London (Lebensmittel); Barry Lewis/Network Photographers/Agentur Focus, Hamburg (Frühstück)

36 Ruth Barker, Plauen (Umfrage); www.kmk.org/pad/sokrates/index.html (Logo)

37 Ruth Barker, Plauen (Frühstück)

40 Nicole Bergemann, Braunschweig (Geldscheine); Ruth Barker, Plauen (3 for 2); Jessica Hatcher, Frankfurt a.M. (Sonderangebot)

42 Interfoto, München (Arcimboldo/Mann); Picture Alliance, Frankfurt a.M. (Arcimboldo/Frau)

43 Valérie Callaghan, Braunschweig (Schwarzes Brett); Jessica Hatcher, Frankfurt a.M. (Holland Park School); Bryn Colton/Assignments Photographers/Corbis, Düsseldorf (Mädchen); Ariel Skelley/Corbis, Düsseldorf (Jungs)

44/45 © Dennis McDonald/Alamy (Schwimmer); Lichtblick-Bildjournalisten, Bochum (Freizeitaktivitäten); Tanja Ripke, Hamburg (Basketball); Lade, Frankfurt (Fahrrad); Reinhard Michaelis, Rosche (Hund, Katze)

46 Ruth Barker, Plauen (Stuhlkreis)

47 Odd Andersen/afp-Bild-Archiv, Berlin (Arsenal Fans); picture-alliance/dpa-Sportreport (Pokal); www.kmk.org/pad/sokrates/index.html (Logo)

50 Michael Rieke, Hannover (Sydney); Roland Witschel, dpa, Hamburg (Pisa); Peter, Gundelfingen (Istanbul); Christian Krug, Münster (Moskau); Kuzmiuk, Silvestris/PhotoPress, Kastl (Warschau); Tanja Ripke, Hamburg (Streetball); Ruth Barker, Plauen (Keyboard, Liegestütze, Pfeifen); Lichtblick-Bildjournalisten, Bochum (Einrad); Andreas Winter, Bremen, www.holiday-kids.de (Pizza)

51 Ruth Barker, Plauen (Umfrage)

53 Schmidbauer, Silvestris/PhotoPress, Kastl (Hamster)

54 Topham Picturepoint, Edenbridge (Pony)

55 Renate Krause, Ettlingen (Zoogeschäft)

56 Reinhard Michaelis, Rosche (Tierärztin); Ruth Barker, Plauen (Waschbär)

57 Kerstin Klemm, Braunschweig (Straße, Straßenschild); Picturefile, David Graham (Zimmer); London Regional Transport (Karte)

62 London Regional Transport (Karte)
63 Kerstin Klemm, Braunschweig (Notting Hill Station); Katharina Cranz, Frankfurt a.M. (U-Bahn)
64/65 HB-Verlag, Hamburg (Oxford Street)
66 Renate Krause, Ettlingen (Kinder)
69 Renate Krause, Ettlingen (Kinder)
71 Renate Krause, Ettlingen (Spiel)
73 Katharina Cranz, Frankfurt a.M. (T-shirt-Stand); Valérie Callaghan, Braunschweig (Marktstand); Jennie Woodcock/ Reflections Photolibrary/Corbis, Düsseldorf (Geburtstag); Topham Picturepoint, Edenbridge (Kantine)
77 Topham Picturepoint, Edenbridge (Kantine); Picturefile, David Graham (Assembly)
82 Michael Jankowski, Braunschweig (Kärtchen); Hans A. Buchbinder (Market Day)
87 Ian Berry/Magnum Photos/Agentur Focus, Hamburg (Kinder beim Ausflug); Dorothee Schade, Papenburg (Aufführung); Action Plus, London (Cricket); J. Walmsley, London (brass rubbing)
88 Lichtblick-Bildjournalisten, Bochum (Rapper); Cinetext, Frankfurt a.M. (Cats)
89 Kentish Town City Farm, London (Logo); Hermera Photo-Objects (Mikrofon); London Aquarium, London (Logo)
94 Action Plus, London (Cricket); Picturefile David Graham (Hockey)/Millbank (Gartenarbeit)
96 Cinetext, Frankfurt a.M. (Cats); Heidolph, Kottgeisering (Planeten); Tina Toase, Oldendorf (Ziege)
99 Dorothee Schade, Papenburg (Theateraufführung)
Innenumschlag hinten: Dr. Peter Güttler, Berlin (Karte)

Textquellen:

16 Ibo Yesil, Hamburg (Schülerarbeit Junge); Melanie Brauns, Plauen (Schülerarbeit Mädchen)
21 "Count up". Text: Tina Toase, Oldendorf/Wetzen; Musik: Christian Vinzentius, Lübeck
27 Stefan Hagendorf, Plauen
32 "The Washing Song". Text: Frank van Ruyssevelt; Musik: Wolfgang Hering und Brigitte Schanz-Hering
56 "Mice" von Rose Fyleman. Reprinted by permission of The Society of Authors (UK).
72 "Spring Cleaning". Aus O!Kay!, der Englischzeitschrift vom FLOH, Ausgabe 4/01. James Delbridge (Musik), Jens Schlieker (Arrangement).
78 "Morning song". Pat Jüngst.
79 "Aunt Ethel's birthday". Renate Krause.
86 Begül Rüzgar, Hamburg (Schulbroschüre)
93 Aylin Ücüncü, Hamburg (Schülerarbeit Outing)
98/99 Abgeänderter Auszug aus "A Knife in the Back" von Dorothee Schade. Schroedel Diesterweg Verlag
99 Maybel Arciaga (Zeichnung)
100 www.penpalworld.com

Nicht alle Copyrightinhaber konnten ermittelt werden; deren Urheberrechte werden hiermit vorsorglich anerkannt.

REPUBLIC OF IRELAND
UNITED KINGDOM
GERMANY
Shetland Islands
Orkney Islands
Outer Hebrides
Isle of Skye
Atlantic Ocean
Loch Ness
Ben Nevis 1344 m
Balmoral
Aberdeen
SCOTLAND
Edinburgh
Glasgow
Tweed
North Sea
NORTHERN IRELAND
Londonderry
Hadrian's Wall
Newcastle